The Pet Professional's Guide to Pet Loss

How to Prevent Burnout, Support Clients, and Manage the Business of Grief

Wendy Van de Poll, MS, CEOL

ISBN: 978-0-9990163-1-2

DISCLAIMER

If you are ever feeling like you can no longer function with your life, become suicidal, and any of the normal grief feelings have become extreme for you, then that is considered unhealthy grief. This is the time to call your hospital, medical practitioner, psychologist, or other health care provider that is trained to help you. Do not isolate yourself if you are experiencing unhealthy grief. Get the professional help that you require.

THANK YOU!

Thank you for purchasing *The Pet Professional's Guide to Pet Loss*. To show my appreciation, I'm offering this special gift to help you prevent and deal with pet loss grief burnout.

To Download Your **FREE GIFT**

Pet Loss Grief Resource Packet

Please Go To:
https://centerforpetlossgrief.com/resource-packet/

This book is dedicated to all the pet professionals who commit their life and passion to help our animals:

Veterinarians
Veterinarian Technicians
Professional Pet Sitters
Dog Walkers
Trainers
Groomers
Rescue Workers
Kennel Owners
Dog Handlers
Behavioral Consultants
Animal Communicators
Barn Managers
Pet Massage Therapists
Pet Physical Therapists
Day-Care Owners
Humane Society Personnel
Foster Parents
Wildlife Rehabilitators
Veterinarian Acupuncturists
Veterinarian Chiropractors
Animal Energy Practitioners
Service Animal Trainers
Prison Dog Trainers/Handlers

Contents

Introduction

As a pet care professional—how many times have you had a client that just received the news their pet is terminally ill, has died tragically, or is dealing with pet hospice? And how many times have you had to deliver the news yourself?

You don't know what to say, but you want to be compassionate and helpful. You are literally either lost for words, feel like you said the wrong thing, or would like to be more effective when delivering the news. Maybe you searched the Internet for help but didn't find the information that would be appropriate for your professional situation.

As a pet care professional, it is critical to have a general knowledge of how to help your clients when they are faced with pet loss grief. With the pet industry growing every day you will be faced more and more regularly with how to address pet loss with grace and compassion.

With this increasing growth in your industry there will be more demands on you and your business. It will be essential to make it a daily practice to take care of yourself. Compassion fatigue and burnout are real, and they both have a way of sneaking up on you.

Dealing with euthanasia, sudden death, dying issues, the loss of pets, and your own grief can upset the balance in your personal and professional life.

This book will give you the background knowledge of the workings of pet loss grief. You will understand what your clients are going through, and you will learn distinct ways to offer them much-needed support. Whether you are a veterinarian, veterinarian tech, dog walker, animal communicator, groomer, or pet sitter, this book will provide you with information on how to offer compassionate support to human clients and at the same time establish healthy boundaries with them.

Because processing your own grief and taking care of your own mental, physical, and spiritual health are so crucial to your professional effectiveness as well as to your overall quality of life, this book supplies specific ways for you, the pet care professional, to do that. Additionally, you will receive guidance to better understand your own beliefs around life and death, an understanding that is pivotal to establish in order to take care of yourself and your clients when dealing with death and dying.

This book is for you if you are a pet care professional that wants to:

- know more about pet loss grief,

- help clients with general grief support,

- know how to manage compassion fatigue,

- avoid burnout, and/or

- add pet loss grief support to your business.

As a pet care professional, pet loss and the grief that comes with it are regular parts of your career. However, that doesn't mean it is easy, and for this reason yours is a profession not suited for everyone. In my experience pet care professionals forget to take care of themselves. Since you are in a caring profession, the desire to help others before you help yourself is a common but detrimental tendency.

The Pet Professional's Guide to Pet Loss was written as a comprehensive guide for all pet care professionals. It is your resource to gain a basic knowledge of—grief and loss, self-care, how to support your clients within your scope of practice, and the business of grief.

As far as I know, there isn't another book like this one available.

I also include a free gift, *Free Pet Loss Grief Resources Packet* that you can access in the beginning of this book or at the book's end in the resource section, and then download from there. This packet has useful "cheat sheets" you can print out to have ready for when you need to access the information quickly.

Along with consulting pet care professionals (see the book's dedication), my personal experiences, plus being a certified end-of-life and pet loss grief coach (CEOL), I have helped countless pet professionals around the world to effectively help their clients and themselves deal with the feelings and emotions of pet loss grief.

I also travel the country teaching my course, *Preventing Burnout During the Pet Loss Grieving Process in Your Practice*. This course is certified by **AAVSB-RACE** to serve the veterinarian profession.

Plus, I offer pet loss grief training programs to veterinarians, humane societies, professional pet sitters, groomers, dog walkers, etc., to incorporate pet loss grief services into their businesses.

All that I offer in this guide I've pulled from my rich experience in the varied roles I've played in regard to working with people about pet loss grief.

Your life has been enriched daily as you interact with your fur, finned, and feathered patients/clients. You may even form meaningful bonds with your human clients. Keep in mind that even as you form these bonds, the cycle of life will have an effect. It is paramount that you nurture and support your personal and professional life appropriately for continued career longevity.

Those that work with animals every day are faced with loss. I have surmised there isn't proper training for pet loss grief support for you or your human clients. I have heard many pet care professionals say the most inappropriate comments, propagate harmful myths about death and grief, and offer support services they are not properly trained for.

My practice is filled with hurting people who are triggered by a pet care professional that meant well but offered the wrong advice—most likely because they weren't educated in the area of pet loss grief.

This book aims to supply you with that much-needed education so that you can wisely and sensitively interact with your clients, and help change for the better the way all pet professionals address death, dying, and grief.

This book will also help you decide the particular level of pet loss grief support you want to incorporate into your business, whether it be general staff sensitivity and awareness training to offering distinct pet loss grief support services. I have seen businesses grow when incorporating grief support.

Louise, a Dog Trainer, Explained—

The best thing about learning about pet loss grief from Wendy is that she really gets grief. She is a pet care professional doing great things and helping us deal with our own grief as well as supplying us with specific tools for helping our clients. Learning from Wendy has even helped grow my business as a trainer. When I go the extra mile and provide compassion in a way that's different from my competitors—my human clients appreciate it, and by word of mouth my business has grown.

I promise that when you read this book, follow the recommendations, and have the downloadable guide at your fingertips, you will be ready to address pet loss grief in a new and better way. You will be able to manage your compassion fatigue and hopefully avoid burnout.

Instead of not knowing what to say or do for yourself or clients, you will have a knowledge base which you can draw from. Whether it's knowing about normal vs. abnormal grief, the eleven destructive myths about dying and grief, the seven stages of grief, what to say and not say, or helping your clients find the appropriate support, you will be ready.

This book is not intended to train you to become a pet loss grief coach or therapist. It takes specific training to do that.

What this book gives is information and techniques so that you can become a more aware, sensitive, and resourceful pet care professional for clients facing and experiencing pet loss and the grief that comes with it.

As a pet care professional, I encourage you to begin reading this book right now, so you can put that new knowledge and the given tools into effect immediately. Each chapter has been crafted to make you into a pet care professional who is more compassionate, knowledgeable, and end-of-life safe.

This book that you are about to read will help you to choose ways to manage pet loss, both that of your clients and your own, with compassion, forgiveness, respect, and love.

The Nature of Grief
Section One

Grief is so human, and it hits everyone at one point or another, at least, in their lives. If you love, you will grieve, and that's just given.

—Kay Redfield Jamison

1. Getting Familiar with Grief

As a pet care professional, you may have experienced many beautiful and loving moments between the people and their animals that are in your care. You have witnessed these moments full of meaning and enduring love that fill the hearts of many on a daily basis. These moments have turned into cherished memories, and they may be the reason why you continue to do the work that you do.

You may have become deeply attached to these animals. You anticipate their visits to your office (or your visits to their home) with great enthusiasm. That's when you get to see how much they've grown or take them on their favorite walk or assess how they're recovering from an injury.

You developed a bonding relationship with these animals. So it comes as no surprise when a client's pet is ill or reached the end of their life—you will understandably experience some level of grief. And this pain can range from a few tears of sadness to raw, nasty, and tough feelings.

Sometimes you may not even be aware of these feelings that are happening to you. As a pet care professional, it is easy to look beyond your grieving process. With running your practice, being a caretaker, and empathizing with the pain and suffering of your patients—you may forget to take care of yourself.

You may then find yourself on the road to burnout—especially with pet loss concerns. Pet loss is a tough business and not something to not pay attention to in regard to yourself. You not only have to take care of yourself, but you may also have an individual client that looks to you for help. If you are not end-of-life safe, meaning you don't have a carefully considered personal plan for dealing with grief, then you are open to a myriad of emotions that could lead to compassion fatigue. When I say "compassion fatigue," I'm referring to when a pet care professional experiences recurring emotional stress and trauma, which then manifests itself as exhaustion. Compassion fatigue is a form of burnout.

This chapter is going to help you learn what normal vs. abnormal grief is, how to recognize both types, and how to begin the process of preventing pet loss grief burnout in the work you love. It will also help you become clear on your own emotions in regard to pet loss grief as well as those of your human clients.

Considerations

When I'm consulting or training pet care professionals with becoming end-of-life safe, the two most frequent comments I hear are "I don't fully understand how to help my clients" and "I can't seem to find the time to take care of myself."

I cannot urge you of this enough: grief is a subject deserving of attention, and you, as a pet care professional, have a responsibility to your clients—and to yourself—to have a foundational knowledge of this issue.

Consider this: when an animal is diagnosed as chronically ill or your client's pet has reached the end of life, there are going to be some very uncomfortable feelings that you are going to feel. There are also going to be emotional stages that your client is going to experience.

Either for you, your client, or you both—these uncomfortable emotions may lead to chaos, anxiety, depression, or even compassion fatigue—which if elicited in you, the pet care professional, could lead to burnout. You may be at a distressing loss for words for what you or your client is going through during this experience.

What are you going to do next for your client?

Your client may be looking to you for the answers. They may be depending on you because you are the professional. However, you find yourself not sure what to say or do next.

Have you heard your clients ask, "Does my sadness ever go away?"? This question is one of the most common I receive in my practice. I would like to answer yes to help them feel better, but I have to give them the honest answer—no, grief doesn't ever go away, but it does change.

What are you going to do for yourself?

Since you are the professional, there is a considerable amount of expectation from your clients. Depending on your profession, your participation in helping them with their pet loss grief will dictate what is ethically appropriate for you to provide (and not provide) to clients.

Coupled with this is the fact that pet care professionals tend to be empathic and dedicated to providing the best care they can for their clients. What this adds up to—when a pet is ill or has died, you naturally find yourself wanting to make it better for your clients.

I have also worked with pet care professionals who are experiencing all levels of burnout in their practice caused by unresolved grief (chapter 7). This is particularly true for veterinarians and their staff who deal with a fair number of euthanasia cases on a regular basis, if not daily.

Case Study—Emily, Certified Veterinarian Technician

Emily has been a vet tech for ten years. Her job is to assist the veterinarian with all euthanasia cases in the practice. She told me she had suffered burnout a few times but hadn't known what it was. Her go-to method for dealing was more exercise and coffee.

Emily dealt with multiple deaths every day. The one thing Emily had going for her was she had a strong viewpoint surrounding death. She understood the profound concept that death brings life and wasn't afraid to talk about it.

Here is what she said to me: "Wendy, I am beginning to hate my job. I can't stand it anymore to be at the side of someone's pet and have to put them to death. I feel like I am executing these animals even though I am acutely aware of the need. I can't sleep anymore, I have anxiety, and I am finding myself depressed."

When I began coaching Emily about the events of her day, weeks, and years of doing the work she loved, she didn't realize her feelings of despair and overwhelm were normal emotions of pet loss grief.

As we continued our work together Emily gained knowledge of her particular feelings and emotions, developed a system of being end-of-life safe, which I will talk about in section 2, and from there she was able to manage her burnout and eventually prevent it from happening again.

Here is what Emily told me at the end of my coaching program for pet care professionals: "Wendy, I can't thank you enough. Now that I know what normal grief is and how to manage my relationship with my patients and myself, I can give the needed attention to those emotions and be more efficient in my job. I understand that I can manage and prevent burnout now because I know how to recognize that grief has a talent for taking over and feeding my compassion fatigue."

When you understand what grief is and by employing the tools for yourself and your clients that I offer in future chapters, you are going to find that you will be able to manage this rough journey with respect, compassion, and knowledge, just as Emily and others did.

When you begin to learn about grief, it is important to know what normal and healthy grief is, and that you understand that each client, office staff, and pet care professional is going to feel something different.

We all have different relationships with the pet(s) in our charge, and each client has a different relationship with their pets. The following will help you understand and support the uncomfortable yet normal feelings in yourself and your clients.

If you or your clients are feeling hopeless because you don't know whom to talk to, how to provide help, or whom to get help from—this is normal grief.

If anger is showing up when you go to work or you are feeling guilty, depressed, numb, or even shock—this is natural for both you and your clients to experience.

Once you understand what normal grief vs. abnormal grief is for yourself and others, the experience will begin to change, both in terms of your expectations and what you can offer your clients. With this understanding your journey will change and become more manageable.

Normal Grief Feelings – A List

Here are some normal feelings of pet grief that you or your clients may experience;

- *Physical*~crying, sobbing, wailing, numbness, dry mouth, nausea, tightness in the chest, restlessness, fatigue, appetite disturbance, sleep disturbance, dizziness, fainting, or shortness of breath

- *Intellectual*~sense of unreality, inability to concentrate, feeling preoccupied with the loss, hallucinations concerning the loss, a sense that time is passing very slowly, or a desire to rationalize feelings about the loss

- *Emotional*~anger, depression, guilt, anxiety, relief, irritability, desire to blame others for the loss, self-doubt, lowered self-esteem, feeling overwhelmed, or feeling out of control, hopeless, or helpless

- *Social*~feelings of isolation or alienation, feeling rejected by others, or reluctance to ask for help

- *Spiritual*~feeling angry at your deity after an animal has died and blaming your deity for the loss, or even bargaining to try and get the animal back

A Life of Its Own

As you can see, normal grief is varied and expansive. The thing about grief is that it has a life of its own. What this means is that you or your client can be going through a quiet period when things feel relatively good. Then something happens, and it triggers an intense, and perhaps unexpected, feeling of pet loss.

I am here to share—pet care professional to pet care professional—let these feelings happen. Let yourself feel what you are going through during your experience.

If you are with a client and they are expressing their feelings of normal grief—let your client do so. Try and resist the urge to make it better for them. Give them the space to express. I will give you tools on how to do this in chapters 5 and 10. But for right now, just listen.

Abnormal Grief Feelings

If you (or you see signs in your client) can no longer function with your life or become suicidal and any of the normal grief feelings become extreme, that is considered unhealthy grief. Now would be the time to suggest to your client to call the hospital, medical practitioner, psychologist, or a health care provider that is trained to help with pet loss.

Get to Know Grief

Step 1: Become Familiar

We have been discussing the necessity of learning what normal grief is, why it is important, and how having this knowledge will help you manage compassion fatigue and prevent burnout.

Being familiar with your own emotional expressions in regard to the daily euthanasia or the periodic death of a pet that may have spent time with you in your kennel, etc., will help you be end-of-life safe in the future.

The normal feelings of grief cannot go unnoticed. When you take the time to become familiar with your personal feelings, work through them, and learn ways to express them in a healthy manner, you will be able to direct your clients in the appropriate direction too.

Step 2: Reach Out

In addition to recognizing your feelings and reaching out for additional support for yourself, a second essential component for helping clients is to know when to suggest they reach out to someone else.

For pet care professionals, I always suggest reaching out to trained individuals who will listen to every word of your conversation, someone that can respect your profession, understand the intricacies of your work, and has the compassion and knowledge to guide you.

For your clients, you can help guide them towards support groups, pet loss grief coaches, and other professionals, but always add to the advice—find someone who will not only listen but also not judge your experience.

Step 3: Spend Time Remembering

In our busy world as pet care professionals, it is easy for us to forget those animals that touched our hearts. I encourage you to spend some time with those memories (chapter 7).

Take note of the times when you think about that particular cat that looked deep into your eyes with gratitude as you proceeded to end their life. Reflect upon your emotions as you remember the dog that lavished you with kisses when they did the perfect sit for their person. Treasure the smile when you remember the parrot that wildly said hello to you when you showed up to feed her while her people were gone.

Yes, grief may come up, but keep in mind that death allows for a particular time to bring you joy with these memories. I will talk about helping your clients with compassionate follow-up in chapter 13.

Step 4: Know Your Grief Feelings

I can't stress enough how important it is for you to know and be familiar with your unique feelings of grief. Everyone grieves differently and with different intensity. Your feelings are going to be with you every day; this is the nature of life.

When I help my pet care professionals and clients understand their grief, it becomes less of a burden or something to fear or dread.

Depending on your profession, you may be dealing with grief during most of your day. For others, it may be periodical.

Whatever your profession—it doesn't matter, death is natural, and it happens to every living being. The more we accept it into our lives as something very powerful, the easier our lives will become, which will allow us to become stellar caretakers for our own emotions as well as for our clients'.

Chapter Wrap-Up

Losing a pet for anyone is tough. They are our beloved patients, clients, companions, teachers, confidants, and best friends. When they physically leave us, they leave an imprint in our hearts.

You heard the story of Emily, the certified veterinarian technician, who found a way to recover and continue her career, even after ten years of suffering from multiple episodes of burnout. Emily learned about her feelings and took the steps necessary to continue with a career she loved.

You've been supplied with a detailed list that described the variety of feelings and tendencies associated with normal grief. In your *Free Pet Loss Grief Resources Packet* (you can access it both in the book's opening and in the resources section, and then download it) you will also find a list of these normal grief feelings. Additionally, we discussed abnormal grief, so you can recognize it too.

You can use these grief descriptions to gain a firm understanding of your own feelings of grief. In doing so, you will hopefully be able to manage compassion fatigue and avoid burnout in your practice. You will then be able to effectively manage your journey of pet loss grief. Plus, you'll be in a position to offer the most appropriate support for your clients to assist them in finding the help they may need.

Spend time with the three *Quick Reference Tips* at the end of this chapter before moving ahead. Remember—be clear and concise with your feelings so that you can work with them as you continue to read this book.

In chapter 2, I am going to teach you the seven stages of grief that you or your clients may or may not experience in full. With each of these steps, I am going to give you examples of what you can expect.

Chapter 1 Quick Reference Tips

1. Making a list of your feelings of grief is one way to begin managing your compassion fatigue and avoiding potential burnout. It will also help you recognize the grief a client may be experiencing.

2. Being familiar with how you are dealing with these feelings will be easier if you arrange your list starting with the most intense feeling and then down to the least charged emotion.

3. Recognizing normal grief is healthy and deserving of attention. Give grief its time for recognition.

2. Navigating the Seven Grief Stages

As I shared in the first chapter, unattended grief can easily lead to compassion fatigue and burnout. It doesn't matter which pet care profession you are in, if left unrecognized, your emotions can lead you to actually leaving a profession you once loved—without exactly knowing the reason why.

Unattended grief can also leave you struggling to understand what is going on so that you possibly end up being impatient with yourself, staff, and clients as they suffer their loss. When you are approaching or experiencing burnout, it is difficult to stay balanced, be kind to others, and support clients.

The other aspect of grief for pet care professionals is—you may also experience your clients struggling to cope with their own unattended grief and expressing that struggle by being irrational, angry towards you, calling the office multiple times a day, or even blaming you for the illness or death of their beloved companion. You may wake up every morning with a headache, dreading going into work and being fed up with the world (or just certain clients) simply because of misunderstanding grief—theirs or your own.

Dealing with pet loss grief for yourself, your clients, and even your employees can definitely take a toll on you professionally, and you may begin to question whether you want to continue with your work.

Keep in mind that whether you are addressing your own feelings or recognizing the grief of your clients—everyone experiences these feelings in different ways and at different stages.

Pet loss grief actually has seven identifiable stages. By understanding these seven stages of grief, your disordered emotions and possible shock about what you are now faced with can change, so you can hopefully feel less stress as you move through these stages.

Learning which stage of pet loss grief you are experiencing is extremely helpful to your coping and healing journey. It can help you not only avoid burnout, but it can also help you be more effective for your clients when they express themselves with varying and quick-changing emotions.

Instead of becoming exhausted, overwhelmed, and even impatient with yourself and/or your clients—in familiarizing yourself with the grief stages, you will gain compassion and respect for the grief journey. This will then allow you to become available to offer the appropriate guidance your client may need at this unique time.

For your clients who are living without their companions, their journey can have many repercussions. Their pet may have been their lifeline or therapy animal. It may have been the only friend they had. Their companion may also have been the focus of their entire life. It is not up to you as the pet care professional to judge and try to change their feelings. It is your ethical duty to respond to their loss with knowledge, compassion, and respect.

You can't do that if you are feeling the pain of pet loss yourself and not doing anything about it. If you try and ignore your own grief emotions, you will become ineffective, tired, angry, and burned out.

I personally have many different ways for being end-of-life safe, which I will talk about in length in chapter 8. What I find extremely important in my own practice is to always have in the forefront of my mind:

- the normal feelings of pet loss grief;

- the stage of grief I, myself, may be in from losing a particular animal client; and

- the stage of grief the deceased animal's person seems to be experiencing.

By exploring the stages of grief in this chapter, you can begin to learn self-compassion and gain a needed understanding of your and your client's journeys.

The grief that you or your client may be feeling right now is perfect, so please be kind to yourself and to them, and don't expect anything more or anything less. It is there, and it's not going to go away. Yet, it will change as time progresses (chapter 4 and 6).

The 7 Stages of Grief

It is extremely helpful to know not only what normal grief is but also the normal stages of grief.

Dr. Elisabeth Kubler-Ross was a pioneer in the hospice movement. While she wasn't a pet grief person, what she discovered can be applied to the journey of pet grief.

In 1969, in her book *On Death and Dying*, Dr. Kubler-Ross made the five steps of grief and/or death well known. The following five steps cover the stages of grieving for the death of a loved one:

- Denial
- Anger
- Bargaining
- Depression
- Acceptance

These five stages became very popular and are recognized widely, mostly as they apply to the dying process. Additionally, people working in this field began to expand on Kubler-Ross's various philosophies and standards. Currently, there are seven stages of grief:

1. Shock and Denial
2. Pain and Guilt
3. Anger and Bargaining
4. Depression, Reflection, and Loneliness
5. Adjustment to Life
6. Your New Normal
7. Acceptance and Hope

Over the years my clients have told me that information on the grief stages is valuable and helps prepare them every day to live more fully and have hope for the future, whether they are pet care professionals or pet lovers.

A holistic veterinarian, Dr. Sara, told me, "I keep the Stages of Grief Resource sheet you gave me in every examining room drawer. I refer to it often, and it helps not only me but also my office staff when supporting people with their animals in hospice, and even at the time of euthanasia. I find knowing these stages of grief helps give a typically chaotic time a little more grace."

This resource sheet is in the *Free Pet Loss Grief Resources Packet* that you can access in the beginning of this book or in the resource section.

Case Study—David, Max, and the Seven Stages

David was a client of mine, and he is not a pet care professional. I am sharing his experience with the seven stages of grief because one of your clients may be experiencing a similar journey. With each of these stages and examples of what David experienced, you will be able to reflect on your own experience with grief and maybe even recognize the experiences of clients.

David experienced all seven stages of grief. He and I started working together three years after Max died. David wanted to get another dog but found he still missed Max.

When David recalled his feelings and actions through our conversations, he felt much better and more in control of what he had experienced and was currently experiencing.

Even still, David was confused and worried because he continued to get angry and impatient whenever his dog walker was telling him that three years was too long to not have another dog and that he should be able to adopt another by now (the length of the grieving period is something we'll address in chapter 3).

Stage 1: Shock and Denial

As we worked together, David began to understand why he felt the unshakable feelings of missing Max and a strong disbelief that Max had died. David recalled during the first 24 hours of being alone without Max, he felt totally in shock and nauseous. He remembered calling his best friend and his friend telling him he would get over it.

David was distressed, upset, and in denial that Max wasn't with him any longer, even three years later. He said to me during one of our calls, "I still can't believe this happened, and I still have hope that it was all a big mix-up and Max will be coming back to me."

Stage 2: Pain and Guilt

David was feeling intense torment and sorrow, so much so that he suffered from various physical issues since Max had died. He went to countless doctors about his "new" shoulder pain, but there was no diagnosis. I assured him that his feelings of anger and sadness were common and in accordance with the second stage of grief.

When this information started to settle in and become more accepted, David understood his feelings better. When he began to forgive himself for any guilt he had, his shoulder pain started to go away.

Stage 3: Anger and Bargaining

When David got angry, he was insistent on blaming himself, his veterinarian, the dog walker, and his spiritual deities. He told me when we began working together that at times he still bargained with them and asked them to give him directions on how to bring Max back, alive.

David told me he went through a stage where he was furious. David explained, "My anger was so intense I found myself going out into the woods and yelling at my deities, my vet, and my dog walker. I even asked the universe, 'If I donate a bunch of money to dog rescue, will you give me Max back?' When you helped me realize that other people experience this and it's common, I didn't feel so angry anymore."

Stage 4: Depression, Reflection, and Loneliness

When David and I started to work together, he was beginning to understand that depression and loneliness were part of the journey. Plus, he was also experiencing memories of Max that were beginning to bring him joy.

Whenever he started to think about Max and the times that they had had together, he felt depressed and very lonely. He told me, "Everyone around me keeps saying that I've been grieving long enough, so I feel like I have to hide my sadness. I don't have anyone that I can talk to. I feel like I have to do this alone."

As we continued to work together, David began to understand that his feelings of loneliness were part of the grief process. After he understood that concept and recognized that his fond memories of Max triggered his sadness and loneliness—he was able to experience his reflections in a different way.

He even shared with me, "I am so glad I can give myself permission every day to not be depressed when I think about

Max. Now that I understand my feelings are normal, I am able to reflect on the times Max and I spent hiking, swimming, and hanging out—with a smile on my face."

Stage 5: Adjustment to Life

Once David began to understand the stages of grief, he began to experience his life in a different way. He recognized when depression, anger, and loneliness were gearing up when he thought of Max. He accepted for the first time in three years that this was normal. David even began to explore the idea of adopting another dog.

He confided one day, "Wendy, I have felt so many crazy and uncomfortable things during these past three years. I am now ready to move on, but I don't want to disrespect my bond with Max. How do I do that?"

This was a great place for David to be in his grief journey, and he posed a question that most of my clients also ask. In all of my books listed in the resource section of this book, I talk about adjusting to a new life in more detail. For now, keep in mind how you can relate your experiences, as well as experiences of your clients, to David and Max.

I have compiled a *Free Pet Loss Grief Resource Packet* that contains a list of the stages of pet loss grief. You can access the free packet at the book's beginning or in the resource section, and download it from there.

Stage 6: Your New Normal

As David adjusted to his life and the changes of not having Max any longer, he began to stop being concerned about what other people thought of him still missing Max and not having another dog yet. He began to adjust to the myriad changes in his new outlook and recognized that he was ready to adopt another dog.

David started to work as a driver at a local organization for black Lab rescue. He enjoyed the volunteer position and three months later adopted another Labrador that had been deemed "unadoptable."

Stage 7: Acceptance and Hope

When David began to experience the last stage of pet grief, he was ready to move forward with an entirely different attitude. He accepted the fact that Max had died and that he had his new dog Riley by his side.

David found his new normal. He was still volunteering and had a bunch of new friends through his service work. Now he could live every day with new adventures with Riley.

This was the stage when he became more aware and accepted his grief stages. He was confident that he could provide everything that Riley needed. He found it easier to make decisions and move through any obstacles for healing.

Did David forget Max at this stage? No, he did not! He was able to recognize that death is something that we cannot avoid and that death does allow for new life and love. Riley and David developed a great bond.

Chapter Wrap-Up

The pet loss grief stages are references to guide you on how you can access and understand your particular position in the pet loss grief journey.

David did experience all the stages of grief. He was able to recognize the stages he was experiencing even three years after Max had died. This knowledge helped him understand those tough stages and be able to appropriately take care of himself. David was able to manage repercussions because he learned not to ignore the emotions and stages he was experiencing.

By reading David's story you will be able to recognize what you may be experiencing—in addition to recognizing the stages of pet loss grief your staff and some of your clients may be going through.

In the next chapter, I am going to teach you about the myths that surround pet grief and how these myths can hold you back from healing. I am also going to show you how you can turn these myths around so that they can help you with your journey, which in turn will help you support your clients.

Chapter 2 Quick Reference Tips

1. Understanding the seven stages of grief will help you prepare for the future.

2. Recognizing the seven stages of grief in yourself first is paramount.

3. There is no "correct" order to experiencing these stages. They can change very quickly, take a long time, or some might not even occur. The same stage can be experienced multiple times for the same loss.

3. Changing the Myths

As a kennel owner, dog walker, groomer, or a member of a veterinarian team, consider yourself to be the perfect role model to help change the myths centered on pet loss grief.

At this point in the book you have an understanding of what constitutes normal grief (chapter 1) and you have explored the seven stages of grief (chapter 2), so we are now going to visit the multitude of myths that come along with pet loss. I am going to share the ten most common myths that I have come across in my practice.

It is important to familiarize yourself with these myths and be ready to help your clients, staff, or even your colleagues when they express one of these myths as a so-called truth. It is also important as a pet care professional to be careful and aware of not starting any new myths.

As a society we have many pre-conceived ideas as to what death is and how we "should" react to it, talk about it, dread it, or accept it (chapter 9). No matter where you are with your beliefs, it is important to approach these myths with an openness and willingness to help not only yourself but your clients as well.

We will approach these myths through Karen, a client whom I coached when she was approaching compassion fatigue. Karen is a wonderful example of a pet professional who was confronted with falsehoods regarding pet loss but who managed to come through to a place of truth and virtue. Karen is a kennel owner, who originally thought it was unprofessional to cry and experience other feelings when clients told her that Fiona, their cat, was chronically ill.

Myth Confrontation: Karen, Kennel for Cats, and Fiona

My client Karen, on our first call, was deeply concerned about her professionalism when her clients came to see her without their cat, Fiona. Karen told me, "When they showed up at my door, I knew something was off. Fiona wasn't in her crate, and Sandy and Bill were not their friendly selves. At first, I thought I'd done something wrong. Then they told me Fiona was dying of cancer. So, I started to cry, but I felt this was wrong because I am supposed to be professional and not show weakness. Plus, I am the one who was supposed to be comforting them, but I was the one crying, so I got it all backwards."

Initially in sharing her story, Karen was horrified and questioned her abilities as a professional. "How could I show my feelings? I should have known better." Karen started to question herself and was even thinking that she needed to get out of her business and do something else. She confided in me that this was not the first time she'd showed her grief in front of a client. She did it every time an animal client died or became ill. She was getting tired and beginning to not enjoy her work.

Then suddenly, as she was explaining this to me, she started to laugh. And just as quickly, she became horrified that she had been laughing, which made her begin to cry. She told me that when she thought about crying in front of a client, it oftentimes made her feel so sad, which then, strangely to her, led to another laughing spell! She felt horrible and confused about the laughter.

My response—"Karen, what you are going through is normal and to feel as if you shouldn't cry or laugh is just a grief myth. In your work of taking care of people's animals, you are going to live out a variety of emotions, and laughter is just one that is going to help you express the overwhelm of grief."

With my guidance, Karen worked to understand and accept that she was going to have a range of feelings, which included laughter. She also learned that tears are not considered a loss of control. She learned that revealing her empathy and sadness through "controlled" tears could be a healing start for herself as well as her clients.

Karen finished her coaching program with me, feeling a lot stronger with her renewed confidence.

Myths about grieving, like the one Karen voiced, have been around for a long time, and they can either really help you with your grief or be a hindrance to your healing process. The key to making these myths help you is to be aware of them, know how you feel about them, and then debunk them.

The Myths

Myth: *It is selfish and extravagant to mourn and grieve the death of a pet when our world has so much human suffering.*

Debunking—You are a pet care professional, and you understand how important pets are for people. You also understand that as a professional, you can easily form bonds with your animal patients and your human clients.

People, whether they are pet care professionals or the general population, are capable of simultaneously grieving both animals and humans. One doesn't detract from the other. Grief, as well as love, isn't "either/or"; it is "both/and."

By grieving and mourning for the loss of your animal patients and/or clients, you are showing tremendous compassion for the world at large. That is a wonderful trait to have. By realizing this, you will stand out from others in your field as compassionate and humane. Plus, at the same time you'll manage compassion fatigue and avoid potential burnout.

Appreciating that your heart is capable of such compassion will give you a tremendous amount of strength to manage and heal your own compassion fatigue, which puts you in a better position to support your human clients as they look to you for support.

Myth: *I must follow the seven stages of grief in their exact order so that I can truly heal my pain.*

Debunking—Grief is not about following a prescribed list. Grief is persistent and can dig so incredibly deep it can and will affect your daily routine. As mentioned in chapters 1 and 2, if you don't pay attention to your emotions, grief will set you up for ultimate burnout and unmanaged compassion fatigue, and for a client who is ignoring their grief, it could leave them feeling hopeless.

However, the last thing that anyone needs to be worried about is following the seven stages of grief in a precise order. Although the stages of grief are extremely valuable, the order in which an individual experiences them varies according to the individual. Let the stages unfold naturally as you become aware of them for yourself or observe them in your clients.

Myth: *There is a right and wrong way to grieve.*

Debunking—As with following the seven stages of grief in chronological order, the same is true about experiencing a unique grief experience—meaning there is not a single correct experience.

Your relationship with your animal patients and/or clients was special to you. No two people or pet care professionals grieve in the same way. While one person may feel sadness, another may feel anger about their patient or pet dying. An individual's grief journey is unique—stick with that for yourself and respect that for your clients!

Grieving is very personal and unique according to the experiences with a beloved companion. It depends on personality, the personality of the animal, the nature of their illness (if they had one) or death, and the grieving individual's coping style, whether that be you or your human client.

Myth: *The best thing to do is to grieve and mourn alone, especially because it is just a pet and pet professionals are not supposed to show grief.*

Debunking—We have been taught that in order to be strong and independent we should not share our grief. It would burden others, and it is inappropriate to let other people know how we are feeling.

That simply isn't true. In fact, when your clients call your office multiple times per day, it is their way of asking for a community. They are merely reaching out for someone to listen to what they are going through.

Having even a little knowledge about normal grief, the stages of grief, and the myths can help you as the pet care professional to support your client in the appropriate way.

When people lose a pet, they oftentimes feel alone because even though our society is changing in terms of the human-animal bond, there is still a stigma surrounding expressing the grief that comes with pet loss.

It is important for not only you but for your human clients to reach out to others who will honestly give support and not judge the grieving process.

You can also grieve as a team if you have staff. It is best to schedule times to get together as a staff to remember those special animals that died each month (more on this in chapter 12). You can have a group debriefing after a particularly difficult death of a pet.

You can help your clients find a support group, a pet loss coach, or an appropriate health care provider. Just be sure the group or person is appropriately trained. We address this more in chapter 11.

Myth: *I have to be "strong" in my grief because I am a pet care professional.*

Debunking—In general, our society teaches that grief feelings can be a sign of weakness, especially grief feelings in regard to animals. This is especially true for pet care professionals who have been taught that it is unprofessional to cry in front of clients during euthanasia or other difficult moments.

Holding back your sadness wreaks havoc on your psyche, but it also does a great disservice to your human clients. You heard about Karen, the kennel owner, who believed it was unprofessional to cry when her clients told her that Fiona was chronically ill. It is not unprofessional to cry. The family wants to know that you've built a relationship with their pet as well.

Feeling sad, frightened, lonely, or depressed are all normal reactions. Crying doesn't mean that anyone is weak. In fact, it takes strength to accept and engage with these difficult emotions and to cry. There have been many times I shared tears with a client because I too was deeply touched by their pet's death.

I encourage pet care professionals to feel those emotions, physical sensations, and spiritual challenges. Showing your feelings will help you and may even help others. By showing your feelings, you are also debunking the first myth about pet loss grief being selfish. When you show your feelings, you are saying, "I have compassion for living beings." And that, my friend, is extremely beautiful!

However, I must add that if your outward expressions of grief are extreme or uncontrollable, it would not be an appropriate or professional course of action to share them with your client. It would be better to express these types of feelings in private or with your professional support team.

Myth: *Grief will go away someday.*

Debunking—Never! Our grief changes as each day goes by. You will never forget that special animal patient or client, yet your feelings of grief will change.

You will also see your human client's emotional state change with time, especially when they share with you the joy of adopting another pet or sharing memories with a smile on their face.

Never feel like anyone has to rush through a grief journey. It takes time. Patience and not judging the length of time come in handy when you are experiencing the stages of grief or working with a client who is doing so.

Your goal for helping yourself or your client is to not support the myth "get over it." We never stop feeling grief for losing a pet. But we learn to move forward in life again with fond memories.

When we move forward, we begin to experience the changing themes of grief (chapter 4) and begin recognizing the new normal (chapter 6).

Myth: *No one gets my pet grief, and I am alone in what I am experiencing.*

Debunking—No one is ever alone with the grief that they are going through. Your client may express this feeling because they don't have the support of family, friends, or coworkers. This puts you in a perfect position for guiding them.

And as a pet care professional, you may also feel unsupported. You may not have a team and be working alone, or your staff, family, and friends can't understand why you should feel awful that you lost a long-time animal client.

People (even pet care professionals and pet lovers) will say unsupportive things, like "There are so many unwanted animals that need homes. See this as an opportunity!" or "At least it wasn't a child."

Even still, there are many, many people who do understand grief. It just may take some time to find the right people to support you or your client in a healthy way. There are supportive friends, end-of-life and grief coaches, and pet loss support groups to walk the journey with. We will talk about this more in section 3.

Myth: *Once I do all the grief work, it will go away.*

Debunking—No matter the person—it takes work to manage grief, compassion fatigue, and burnout. Even after doing the necessary work during the grieving process, grief can come up again. It is not uncommon to have deep feelings of grief appear even years later. It is normal for this to happen, and as pet care professionals you can be frequently reminded of this.

Your client's cat was really special to them. Your client's dog that sat in front of you with a huge smile every time you saw them was special for you. It is important to let the emotions of grief to happen.

If you feel like these emotions will go away without working on them, you are only stuffing them in and setting yourself up for burnout. The grief will still change, but it may take longer. This could lead to you not learning grief's powerful lessons, which could then lead to you finding yourself no longer able to do the work you love.

And as many of my clients say, "Grief has a great talent of surprising you when you least expect it." So it is better to actively acknowledge, process, and experience it than to stuff it down only for it to pop up at surprising times and in unwelcoming forms.

Myth: *Having feelings of relief is not good.*

Debunking—Here is the thing—your client's companion has died; you may have even performed the euthanasia. Their pet was maybe very sick, elderly, or suffered an accident, so keeping them alive was not an option.

Karen asked me during one of our sessions together, "Is it normal for me to feel a sense of relief when Fiona died?" It is okay to experience moments of relief, even when you are grieving about a pet's illness or death. It is healthy and doesn't mean you are forgetting the pet's situation or disrespecting them.

Fiona was extremely ill and suffering. I encouraged Karen to see any relief she felt in regard to Fiona's death as a compassionate expression as well as her body's way of giving her a breather from stress, pain, and anxiety. It is a survival mechanism that we do not need to fear. Relief is a first-aid mechanism.

Myth: *It is horrible to feel happy that my patient/client died.*

Debunking—If you had an animal patient or client that was suffering, there may be a little place in your mind that feels happy and even joyful once they died.

If this is so, when the time has come and your patient/client has reached the end of their life, you may feel relieved and even slightly glad. This is a very common feeling for my clients that suffered the pain and angst of losing an animal to terminal illnesses.

When your animal patient is in pain and suffering every day, it can take a lot out of you, professionally, emotionally, physically, and spiritually. When you experience the animal's person waiting for the "perfect time" to choose euthanasia for their animal, however they wait too long, it can break your heart and leave you feeling hopeless and helpless.

While performing euthanasia, hearing the news about the death of a client, or, like in Karen's case, hearing news of an animal patient's death—feeling slightly glad is a very normal feeling of grief. Keep in mind that this is not due to selfishness, but it is simply a recognition that your patient is no longer suffering in the physical world.

Chapter Wrap-Up

These grief myths are very common, and many people think they are true. It is up to you as the pet care professional to debunk them and help not only yourself but also your clients understand how ineffective they are.

These myths, in conjunction with inappropriate comments (more on these in chapter 5), can easily trigger grief. If you are not aware of the myths, you may become confused as to why suddenly you or your client is feeling sad or very angry.

Even though they may be well-meaning colleagues, friends, family, or coworkers, when one of them offers you a myth as a so-called "word of wisdom," it can pack a powerful punch to trigger pet loss grief.

However, once you become aware of these myths and why they are not true, you will be able to react to them with grace and compassion for yourself and your clients, and manage potential compassion fatigue and burnout.

Here is the thing about believing these myths and letting them affect you—I have seen in my practice that when folks believe and live by these myths, they get stuck in their grief and have a difficult time gaining personal peace.

When they learn to recognize these myths, debunk them, and replace them with positive thoughts and actions, they are able to spend more time loving their pets that have died and, in the case of pet care professionals, offering the right kind of support to grieving clients, rather than being stressed out by unknown anxiety.

I have included a copy of these myths in your *Free Pet Loss Grief Resources Packet* that you can find at the beginning or in the resource section of this book, and download it from there.

In chapter 4, you will learn about how grief changes and why it is important to establish expectations and anticipate how you are going to handle these changes. In doing this, you are preparing yourself for daily compassion fatigue, which in turn helps you navigate your grief journey, avoid burnout, and offer the best support you can for yourself and your clients.

Chapter 3 Quick Reference Tips

1. Shedding myths surrounding pet death will give you effective support and a tool for helping clients.

2. Honesty does not create a myth. Honesty creates truth, and our clients expect that from us.

3. When myths trigger grief, it gives a chance for honesty and creating an open dialogue with clients when sharing stories about their pet.

4. Changing Themes of Grief

A crucial point about grief to address is it has a beginning and a middle. Yet, truthfully, grief does not have an end. As humans we would like grief to never happen, avoid it, and not deal with it. But we can't, we must change daily as we experience its metamorphosis.

Knowing that grief never ends can easily cause fear and panic in anyone experiencing pet loss. It challenges your hope and happiness. It can take time, energy, and work to believe that change will eventually happen.

When you have the knowledge and the tools to manage this characteristic of grief—the fact it changes and never really ends—you will be able to be clear with yourself as to what is happening, as well as understand where your client is in their journey.

In the previous chapters I've described many aspects in regard to the grief journey. It is essential that as a pet care professional you prepare for what is to come—not only to support yourself but to guide your clients in the most appropriate way.

Whether that be the common and incorrect myths (chapter 3), the seven stages of grief (chapter 2), appropriate comments to say to clients in grief (chapter 5), avoiding burnout (chapter 8), or now—what to expect when grief changes, I want to give you as many tools as I can, so you feel supported with managing compassion fatigue. When you know what to expect and how to be prepared, it can be a relief when your client expresses their grief or when you recognize your own.

In general, as a pet care professional you are going to confront the changing nature of the grief journey whether you are dealing with death every day or once in a while. Change is something you can depend on, and being patient with knowledge is the best advice I give you.

Case Study—Katharine, Dog Groomer

Katharine had been a dog groomer for five years before she figured out what was going on with her. She called me because she was experiencing some feelings that she was unsure of and it was making her uncomfortable.

A previous client was coming back to her with their new dog. Their first dog, Emma, who was also Katharine's first grooming client, died after three years from cancer. Katharine loved Emma because Emma represented the beginning of her business, and Katharine had fond memories of Emma's mischievous antics. She looked forward to Emma coming in every month.

When Katharine called me, she was nervous about how to communicate with these clients. Although she still thought of Emma and missed her, she also found herself giggling when she was reminded of one of the dog's antics. Katharine was concerned about her joy and didn't want to do or say anything inappropriate with her clients and their new dog.

Katharine found that by knowing what to expect on the grief journey, she could deal with the multitude of changes that happened in her life, as well as her clients'. When her clients showed up with Gracie, Katharine felt prepared as a compassionate pet care professional.

Katharine shared—

> At first, I had no idea what was going on with my emotions. I figured my sadness for Emma had ended. I didn't realize I would feel grief again when my clients called and wanted to make an appointment for Gracie. I was concerned, and I didn't want to do or say something I would regret later. I wasn't sure what to do with the fact my grief was back and that I was experiencing joy and happiness along with the sadness.
>
> Wendy, you helped me understand that grief changes. You helped me to understand that and how to be aware of any changes my clients may have experienced as well.
>
> Even though I was not looking forward to the day when they brought Gracie to my shop—when they did, we all had a wonderful time with sharing memories. They told me the story about how they realized that it was time to share their lives with a new dog, so they adopted Gracie.
>
> My fear was real, but after you helped me recognize that grief never ends but changes over time, I was able to manage my fear with many clients and share with them fond memories.

Katharine's experience helped her understand how important it was to know what to expect. It helped her remember that her grief journey was unique to her, and it was also normal. With this knowledge she was able to proceed as she wished with her grieving experience and become a better pet care professional.

Possible Changes

Here are some of the unexpected things that Katharine experienced that you or you clients may or may not experience as your grief changes over time.

You and your clients may become aware of . . .

- different and unexpected changes in life and your business;

- a time when the full extent of loss is felt;

- ways to redefine the relationship that you have with your human client and your client with their pet;

- new discoveries of some areas of personal/business growth through your pet grief; and/or

- joyful memories of times you shared together with your animal client and the memories shared by your human client as they continue having you work with their other pets.

Remember, this can be a very challenging time period for anyone—you the pet care professional or your client. Feeling both the extent of the loss as well as the emergence of new feelings of grief can trigger old feelings of grief (chapter 7). It is difficult for many during this stretch of time to recognize and accept how life is changing. In chapter 6, I will be sharing in more detail how to recognize the "new normal" of pet loss, and you'll get tools to help you manage.

As a pet care professional, you will observe your human clients experiencing and learning who they are without their pet. They will be moving into a phase of discovering and understanding life without the physical presence of a beloved companion. And you, as the pet care professional, will be responding to them in a different manner as well.

Your human client may seek out a new groomer, veterinarian, kennel, etc., simply because the memories are too painful to continue doing business with you.

They may begin to think about getting another pet or volunteering at a local humane society.

Then when they return to your business, you may even witness feelings of relief, which is perfectly normal. If an animal client was very ill and suffered a lot during the end of their life, you too may feel relieved as a professional that the animal is no longer suffering, and you may feel happy that your human client made a choice to euthanize. This, too, is a natural feeling to have.

There are many things that will happen during this stage of pet loss grief, and its unfolding will be unique to everyone.

Please use the three *Quick Reference Tips* to help you prepare for these changes and to establish the action plan that you can take to heal your pet grief.

Chapter Wrap-Up

As with the other parts of the grief journey, it is important to establish expectations and anticipate how you are going to handle your emotions and decisions. In doing this, you are preparing yourself, which in turn helps you navigate your grief journey, manage compassion fatigue, avoid burnout, and offer the best support you can for your clients.

After a pet dies, there will be many changes to keep in mind. Changes in the way you relate to your human clients, your staff, and to various personal and professional events in your life. Being aware of these changes will be helpful and will be a valuable tool for you to remain healthy.

Keep in mind, since grief is a living and breathing entity—certain parts of the grief process will remain constant even though others will change. We will discuss that in more detail in section two.

The next section is dedicated to you, the pet care professional. I will guide you to understanding your own beliefs surrounding the end of life and how to deal with the loss of life. You will learn how to be end-of-life safe and how to recognize your own feelings of grief. When you take care of yourself, you will learn to manage compassion fatigue and stop burnout before it happens.

Chapter 4 Quick Reference Tips

1. Grief has a beginning, a middle, but never an end.

2. Grief will change and its metamorphosis can change how you view your business and your clients' experiences.

3. Being prepared for the changing themes of grief will help you understand what you and your clients are going through.

Caring for Your Client and Yourself
Section Two

Take a rest, a field that has rested gives a bountiful crop.

—Ovid

5. Knowing What to Say When

An important thing to remember as a pet care professional is to be aware of what you are saying to your clients. When you are busy, running late, or a bit preoccupied with a personal matter that's mulling in your mind, it can be incredibly easy to say something to your client that you may regret later.

As a pet care professional, you already know that you will lose animal clients due to accidental death, longer-term illnesses, and old age, despite your best efforts and compassion. As you know from reading section 1, you are then exposed to the emotions of the families. In this section you are going to learn about ways to become more aware of yourself in terms of death and dying.

As we've already established, people's experiences are unique and different, as are their reactions. You must respect that everyone, including you, grieves and mourns in their own time and way. It is imperative that you are aware of this, so you can support your client through this time.

If you are uncomfortable with a client's expression of grief—which is normal—it is easy to say or do something that is cliché, triggers their grief, and/or elicits an uncharacteristic response that you may find even more discomfiting.

Of course, you want them to feel better, but your saying things without thinking or doing things without being aware sets you on the straight track to compassion fatigue and eventually burnout.

Here are three common and important ways to prepare for sensitive and potentially emotionally-charged interactions with human clients who are facing pet loss.

Taking Care of Yourself First

1. Before you see a client to deliver or receive difficult news, find a quiet place and calm your mind and gather yourself. If there is no quiet place to be found, simply take a moment and breathe. You do not need to feel as if you have to talk and say something right away.

2. Acknowledge the loss for yourself. Ask yourself before you speak with your client, "How do I feel about losing Gus?" Even if it is an emergency situation, there is still time for you to quietly acknowledge how you feel before you say anything to the client.

3. Listen to your human client and wait—then listen again. This requires skill and patience. When, as a pet care professional, you actively listen to a client's story, it requires you to hear what they are saying without judgment or interruption. By doing this you are showing you care. You are also taking care of yourself because you are not trying to "fix" their grief (chapter 11).

Respect yourself, so you can respect your client. If you are busy or dealing with high emotions with a client, it is still important to focus on them. However, if you don't have boundaries or outlets for fun and balance, you will not be prepared at such moments (chapter 8). When you are able to remain calm and maintain eye contact, it becomes easier and less burdensome to give support.

Becoming aware of how you take care of yourself and what you say and do has a double benefit. Your effectiveness and sensitivity to your clients becomes less draining, and your longevity is increased for the work you love to do.

However, how do you know what to say to a client that is appropriate and how do you acknowledge the loss? Shortly, I'm supplying you with five recommendations on what to specifically avoid saying to clients who are facing pet loss. These five recommendations are not an exhaustive list, yet they are the most common and helpful in my experience.

Let me add that there are likely many other particular things to avoid saying. In my practice I keep discovering new ones as I work with different clients. In fact, as you read my five particular recommendations, you may have some of your own that you can add to the list.

Keep in mind—you may not agree with all of them and think, "Really Wendy? Of course, I wouldn't say that!" Yet, I have heard pet professionals say each and every one of the five common statements below—even to me as their client!

The Task

Before I share the most common statements of what not to say, I would like to address that careful balance of being helpful and compassionate to clients vs. triggering their grief. You want them to know you care, yet you also need to be mindful and say things that are helpful and well meaning, rather than potential triggers for grief.

What happens when you say these unintentionally unsupportive things is that you are inadvertently fueling and activating their grief. In turn, this sets up a potentially charged emotional environment that you may feel like you need to fix, which becomes overwhelming for both you, the pet care professional, and the client. I can assure you compassion fatigue and burnout are guaranteed to be on the way when this difficult chain of events gets activated.

It is normal for people to say unsupportive, yet what they think are well meaning, things to someone who has lost a cat, dog, horse, hamster, or even a goldfish. Yet keep in mind, your words can hurt and can actually trigger grief.

Now here is the thing—as a society we have gotten very distant from the dying process. We view it as something to be afraid of, and we may even want to avoid it (chapter 9). As people, the more we accept death and allow our grief to happen in a safe environment, then the healthier this process will be.

I am going to teach you in this chapter how you can use what you've learned about grief itself (chapter 1), the stages of grief (chapter 2), and changing the myths (chapter 3), so you can be prepared for knowing what to say during a highly emotional time for your human clients.

Case Study—Dr. Steven, Veterinarian

Dr. Steven owns a very busy practice. He loves his work, his staff, and his patients. During our first appointment, Dr. Steven expressed a healthy view on death and dying.

He called me because he wanted to do better—not only for his staff and human clients but for himself as well. Dr. Steven made it very clear that he was concerned for his clients' welfare. He wanted, for himself as well as his staff, to learn how to be compassionate, professional, and well versed in what to say when an animal patient was diagnosed as terminally ill or needed to be euthanized.

We worked on this for a few weeks, and I spent the day with his staff teaching them about how to avoid burnout and manage compassion fatigue, which most of them were feeling at varying levels.

I even observed them in action—and for the most part, they were fabulous. They respected their clients who were experiencing shock or disbelief. They never appeared rushed or abrupt. And I observed their treatment of the pets was gentle, soothing, and careful—even after euthanasia.

I also noticed that when the staff forgot I was observing, unintentional yet inappropriate comments snuck through. Even though Dr. Steven's staff was extremely well meaning, here is what I heard: "I know how you feel" or "Our pets never live long enough." I even heard: "There are so many cats at the shelter right now—you can get another."

Words can hurt, and they can cause a client to go farther down the grief process. The beautiful result from my time spent with Dr. Steven and his staff is that they were willing to learn, change, and retrain themselves. They saw the benefit of learning the appropriate things to say to a grieving client.

When I checked in with Dr. Steven four months after his office finished working with me, he shared, "Wendy, when you taught us about crafting appropriate comments, we realized that we had not been helping our clients. We, in fact, were causing them more stress, which made us feel less compassionate and ineffective. Now we are able to manage the stress in our office for ourselves and our clients much better."

Here are a few of the many statements that I worked on with Dr. Steven and his staff.

Hurtful Things to Avoid Saying

Your pet had a great life, and you gave them all you could.

We all have said this, right? I used to before I became knowledgeable and until I saw how much it really didn't help my friends. It was a statement that only offered a very temporary sense of relief or joy. After saying this and hearing this said by other pet care professionals, I witnessed something very interesting: anger, depression, anxiety, etc., would increase to an even more intense level.

This statement doesn't help your client feel supported in the long run. Pet parents have unique relationships with their companions, and no two are alike. This comment can be devastating and trigger tremendous guilt.

When a client is expressing grief, and you respond by saying, "Your pet had a great life, and you gave them all you could," essentially you are shutting them down, closing down any space for their talking and feeling. Instead, just listen and not say anything when your client is expressing guilt over euthanizing and what they might have done better for their pet.

Why?

Because your client just wants someone to listen.

I am so sorry to hear that.

This one is a big one, one you may not agree with, and the most popular thing to say when we either get the news a client's pet has died or we have to give the news to a client. The fact is this statement suggests that it is somehow your fault the pet died or it puts the focus of the pet's dying on you and your sorrow. In fact, it is not your fault that the pet reached the end of their life. And it is the client's feelings, not your sorrow, that the focus really should be on. In saying, "I am sorry . . ." it's likely your client will feel as if they have to take care of you and offer their support in regard to your sorrow!

I know it may be a moot point, but a kinder, more supportive, and compassionate way to respond to this type of news is "I am so sad to hear that Gus died. Would you like me to just listen to what you are feeling?" This type of comment will give your client a safe place to express their grief rather than feeling like they have to take care of your sadness, feel responsible for your sadness, or protect themselves from feeling even more grief.

This alternative comment will also help you be end-of-life safe and help you manage your own grieving from losing this particular animal client (chapter 6, 7, 8, and 9).

How are you doing?

"How are you doing?" is commonly used yet well worn. Your client may feel pressured to feel better than they actually are if you say this to them. You may find them answering, "Fine," "Okay," or even, "Great."

When you say to a client, "How are you doing?" they may hear something completely different, like "Please tell me that everything is fine with you because it is uncomfortable if you say you are sad."

When you have a client that you haven't seen for a while or you just get the news, you can say to them instead, "It's tough for you right now."

It is important to let your client know that you are acknowledging that what they are experiencing right now is painful and difficult.

The most important thing is to let your clients have a chance to grieve without judgment, even if "How are you doing?" doesn't seem like a pressuring, judgmental question to pose to them. A grieving person often hears something completely different.

You can always get another . . .

This is another tough one. When we see people hurting, our nature as professionals is to want to make it better for them. A quick response to give a client is "You can always get another dog. There are so many that need new homes." However, if you say this, it sounds to your client like you are suggesting their beloved companion is replaceable and that the grief they are feeling isn't justifiable.

This comment can easily trigger their pain of loss and desperation. Your client will be led to feel that they will somehow forget their pet if they "replace" it with another—

and that they should forget their pet because it is replaceable.

A supportive response would be "Please tell me about your pet."

When people are grieving, they oftentimes cannot look forward to the future. Some of the best support you can give your clients is when you let them share their memories and just listen to them without suggesting solutions.

This all happens eventually. All things must die.

Yes, this is true. Everyone experiences grief and death. Loss is part of life. Yet, when we say this to someone who is experiencing pending loss or loss itself, it minimizes the actual loss at that moment and minimizes the person's tremendous grief.

A better thing to say is "You must really miss your pet."

When you focus on the reality of the loss rather than minimizing it as a non-negotiable aspect of life, you will be much more effective in helping your clients.

Chapter Wrap-Up

This chapter is aimed at helping you become aware of the unsupportive things that you might say when your client is coping with pet loss. These common statements can easily trigger their grief in a way that you may be unprepared for.

The key is to think about those statements and replace them with the alternatives I offered above. Your main goal as a pet care professional is to offer appropriate support and help people feel accepted and not judged for their emotions and actions.

You can prepare yourself by learning more about grief (chapter 1) and its seven stages (chapter 3). You can use this chapter's *Quick Reference Tips* to best prepare yourself to offer positive support to clients, which in turn will positively benefit you and the longevity of your career.

Knowing what to say when and taking care of yourself first are chief for lessening your stress. It is always difficult to be 100% there for your clients. The only way you can do this is to be aware of your own actions and choice of words.

In your *Free Pet Loss Grief Resources Packet* you will also find a list of appropriate comments. If you've not yet downloaded it, you can find it at the beginning of this book and in the resources section.

In chapter 6, I am going to help you recognize the "new normal" of grief, both for yourself and your client. It can be a confusing and possibly challenging time for you as you try to navigate your own feelings, but you will reach a new normal.

Chapter 5 Quick Reference Tips

1. Before you respond to your client's grief—take a breath and never judge.

2. Never be in a rush when saying something to a client coping with pet loss.

3. Listen to your client. You don't have to say a thing. Remember to wait before you say something you may regret later.

6. Recognizing the New Normal

Grief is complicated and has so many facets. As discussed, accepting grief is part of the process. Additionally, working on recognizing what happens in the future is a significant part of your journey as a pet care professional.

I am going to address a juncture of grief that you may notice as time progresses that can also be confusing. This juncture is called the "new normal." It is valuable for you to understand the intricacies of this aspect of the grief journey so that you can be end-of-life safe and offer the best possible support to your clients.

Whether you decide to immerse yourself in the study of pet loss grief coaching (chapters 11 and 12) or you just want to know the highlights—recognizing the "new normal" stage will help you navigate your journey as well as you clients'.

As a pet care professional committed to doing the work necessary to manage and avoid the buildup of grief emotions, you will experience greater control within your work when you are better able to identify the intricacies of the "new normal." You will offer stellar support for yourself, your staff, and your clients—when you recognize the "new normal."

What Is the "New Normal"?

Once someone you love has died, life is different from anything you have known before. Your identity, daily activities, and sense of purpose are different. This different, changed life is what I mean by the "new normal."

We will explore what you, as the pet care professional, can expect when you or your human clients experience the grief associated with pet hospice and/or the end of a pet's life, and reach the juncture of the "new normal." There will be examples and a case study illustrating how life changes after a pet dies and how someone copes with these changes to find that "new normal."

Let's begin with a case study in which we learn about Sara, an equine massage therapist. We will hear about her discovery of a "new normal" through the journey of one of her favorite horses.

Case Study—Sara, Equine Massage Therapist, and Firefly

Sara was an equine massage therapy colleague of mine whom I had known for a very long time. She hired me after she began experiencing a very difficult time with the death of Firefly.

This horse was extremely special to Sara. She had known him for 20 years. He was one of her study horses during massage school. She went with him to shows and was there at a moment's notice when he needed her care. Sara also developed a mutual and professional relationship with Firefly's people.

Every week Sara and Firefly had a routine. She would come to the barn, spend some time just chatting with him, and offer him the hands-on treatment that they both enjoyed. It was clear they had a special bond. Firefly's people noticed this and appreciated it as well.

Sara shared during one of her coaching sessions, "Now, when I pull into the farm but there's no Firefly running to greet me—it's devastating to me. I'm finding it hard to continue my work there. When I do, I feel like I'm disrespecting the needs of the other horses because I'm so aware of Firefly's absence. But then I also feel like I'm disrespecting the bond I shared with Firefly because I'm working with those other horses like everything is fine. I'm getting tired of people around me telling me that I have been sad long enough and I need to get back to the barn."

Here is the thing about what Sara was experiencing—everything that she said is considered normal grief. She experienced a huge loss in her life. Though the act of articulating what she felt was challenging, Sara was beginning to discover her "new normal."

When Sara was ready, I shared with her the following five steps to help her feel supported in discovering her "new normal." Hopefully they will help you as well with what you are experiencing in your business and to help you recognize what some of your clients may be going through.

Recognizing the Facets of the New Normal

A New Identity

After a pet dies, life and daily routines are going to change for your client. You will notice they are not the same person whom you were accustomed to. Those regular daily, weekly, and yearly activities they had with their pet are no longer happening, and they will have extra time on their hands.

Since they no longer have a physical relationship with their pet, and depending on the degree of trauma in regard to their pet's death, there is a possibility they will develop a different set of beliefs and thoughts as a result. This is something to be aware of as a professional as it might affect you.

Your client may come in with a new pet and display behavior that you are not familiar with. They may be struggling with finding ways to relate to their new companion, or they may still be trying to navigate feelings of grief.

Your "new normal" in relation to this client is to not expect them to be who they were before in their personality; to not expect they are going to treat their current companion in the same way they did with the companion you knew. They may be adopting a totally new diet, treatment, and protocol for their new companion. Without judgment or question you need to allow them these changes.

A New Relationship with the Pet That Died

Many of my clients work on a common goal—to not forget their deceased pet but to change the relationship from a physical presence to one of wonderful memories or to a spiritual relationship.

Many of my pet care professional clients do the same thing. They hold monthly life celebrations to remember the animals in their care. They have a memorial board in their offices and dedicate time to remembering patients and animal clients that were in their care.

By giving yourself the space and time to form this new identity or "new normal," one that does not include your special animal clients in the same way as when they were living, and by allowing yourself to enjoy memories, you will begin to have a new relationship with your loved ones that have died. You'll find that this new relationship offers you a beautiful and healthy way to take care of yourself.

A New Group of Friends

Even though we live in a society that loves our animal companions, there are some people that don't understand or respect the fact that losing a beloved animal is extremely painful. This could be a difficult time for your client because they may feel alone with their grief and look to you to fill that void.

Your clients' friends may no longer support them because those friends became impatient with their grief process. The client will then possibly look to you for some kind of support.

On the other hand—you, as the pet care professional, may not have your own support system, and this will be the time for you to reassess your boundaries. If you don't reach out to the appropriate professional when you need it, you could easily find yourself in a situation where you are seeking support from your client. This is not an appropriate boundary.

A New Sense of Purpose

A common feeling that my clients go through is that after a beloved animal has died, they question their purpose in life. Sara did this when Firefly died. She actually thought about giving up her equine massage practice because she felt like

Firefly was a vital part of it and without him there was no purpose in her work.

Like Sara, you may be experiencing the same thing; you realize how much you depended on the physical presence of a particular animal to offer you happiness and stress relief. The animal client helped you shape a routine and also played a crucial role in managing your stress with a busy practice. Now that the animal client has died, you may be questioning the effectiveness of your work. This is common and understandable for 90% of the pet care professionals I have worked with.

Many people realize new life purposes and make significant life changes after their beloved companions die. For example, some decide to volunteer at local humane societies, start rescue groups of their own, or choose an entirely different set of friends. After Firefly died, Sara started a fund for rescue horses. You or your human clients may do something similar.

A Celebration of Your Growth

Grief gives you a way to explore how life changes and what you learn will greatly depend on how you or your client views life and death (chapter 9).

Grief is usually unwanted or unplanned. However, the journey of grief can also be a wonderful experience for personal evolution.

When you celebrate how you and your office staff have grown from having shared your hearts and souls with various animal companions, it can help you realize the beautiful and rich experience that your practice contributes to all those involved. It can also help you learn how comfortable you can feel in your new normal.

Some of my clients learn how to be more sensitive to others from living through their own pain due to the loss of their companion. Others decide to share their hearts and give back to animals in need. Some learn to celebrate the gifts that their animal patients gave them, so they live their lives in completely different ways.

After Sara worked through these five steps and discovered a different way of dealing with her grief, she was then able to move forward with a different sense of how her personal and professional life had changed. She eventually began to feel more confident with her unexpected feelings of joy and happiness.

Did Sara's grief go completely away? No, it did not, but it changed and wasn't as controlling. She was able to go to the barn and share memories with Firefly's people.

Sara admitted to me at the end of her coaching program, "I never thought I would be able to survive in my profession after Firefly died. He was my first horse in school, and we shared so much together. He was my pal, and not having him run up to my truck when I arrived for his massage devastated me. When he died, I couldn't even talk to his people. But when I explored these five steps on my own time, I was able to realize that what I was feeling was normal, and my life was going to be okay. I even shared the five steps with Firefly's people, and it helped them too."

Sara's experience helped her understand how important it was to know what to expect. It helped her remember that her grief journey was unique to her and normal. With this knowledge she was able to proceed as she wished with her grief journey—by helping herself first and then Firefly's people.

Surprising, Potent Knowledge

Here are some unanticipated things that Sara experienced that you may or may not experience in your business.

You or your client may become aware of:

- some different and unexpected changes in life;

- a time when the full extent of the loss is felt;

- ways to redefine your relationship with the deceased pet;

- new discoveries of some areas of personal growth through pet grief; and/or

- the joy felt when sharing memories of the pet with others.

Remember, this can be a very challenging time for anyone. The extent of your loss is felt, and new feelings of grief will emerge. It is important that you recognize this, so you don't feel as if you need to fix yourself or your client, or give advice. Remember, grief is a journey. For your clients, it is their journey. But it is yours too—so take care of yourself.

The Manifestation of a New Normal

During this critical juncture, you or your client will begin to recognize how life is taking on new directions—new thoughts, decisions, routines, friends, weekend activities, and changes in outlook.

You may move into a phase of discovering your new normal by taking steps to make your practice/business more end-of-life safe. Your client will move towards understanding a "new" life without the physical presence of their pet.

You may learn to take care of yourself by eating right, getting enough sleep, and making time to exercise to provide yourself with the stamina to cope with daily stresses. You may also decide to spend more time outdoors, which can be a great stress reducer.

Your client may begin to think about getting another pet and look to you for help. They may volunteer at a local humane society.

Your attitude may change, and you can expect the best. When you begin to think positive thoughts and spread your newfound optimism—you will experience changes for yourself and those around you. Try and look at grief as an opportunity to grow and prioritize what is important in your life. Allow yourself to feel joy if that is what you are experiencing in that moment.

If your client's pet died suddenly or unexpectedly, this could present an entirely different experience and process. Be patient as this type of trauma takes time to process, and your client may not be ready to discover their new normal yet.

Remember, there are many things that will happen during this stage of pet loss and grief. Again, the journey will be unique to the individual experiencing grief, depending on many facets at play in the individual's life.

Like grief in general, there will be no prescribed timeframe. The relationship, the pet care professional, and the human client all experience something different, and that will never change.

When you or your client experiences a new normal, everyone will be able to continue to acknowledge and honor their grief, which certainly will resurface. This is what grief is about—it has a life of its own. Yet, during this stage, everyone will be able to recognize and celebrate growth and gains as well!

Chapter Wrap-Up

The new normal is a crucial juncture in the grieving process that is not to be ignored. This juncture is worthy of understanding because it can also be confusing.

The intricacies of the new normal can be subtle or apparent. Recognizing them will lend to your career longevity, your being end-of-life safe, and your being able to offer the best you can for your clients.

Please revisit the five steps for discovering the new normal to help you recognize what is going on with yourself and your clients. These steps will assist you by giving you more self-awareness to make the best business and personal decisions.

Each time you review the steps, you will learn, process, and understand something new that can be implemented into your daily journey. Know that you will feel out of place at times, confused, and frustrated—and that is okay—you now have the tools to cope with that.

The journey of pet grief is unique to everyone. Honor your and your clients' journeys with respect and dignity. No one can alter that if you are aware of and accountable for your process.

Use the chapter's *Quick Reference Tips* to help you be prepared for your new normal and the action that you can take to manage potential compassion fatigue.

In the next chapter, I stress the importance of recognizing and dealing with all losses in life so that you can be healthy when confronted with new death and grief experiences.

Chapter 6 Quick Reference Tips

1. The "new normal" is an indispensable juncture for your client. It is also integral to know what to expect from your clients and yourself at this juncture. This facet of grieving is vital for healing.

2. Each client will discover their own unique "new normal." No two people experience it the same. Keep this in mind as you think of your own ways of discovering your new normal in regard to a client.

3. There is no timeframe for reaching a "new normal." Some clients will discover it quickly; others will take weeks, months, and even years. It will be important for you to not have expectations when communicating with them.

7. Dealing with Past Losses

Thus far in this book we've focused on the intricacies of pet loss grief, what to be aware of within yourself and in your clients, and the tools to help you manage compassion fatigue and avoid burnout.

Since loss occurs in your personal as well as professional life, I would also like to stress the importance of recognizing, coming to terms with, and understanding some of the most common losses.

The purpose of this chapter is to help you begin to explore how you are affected by the various losses in your life in order to enable you to help your clients in a healthy manner.

I have seen in my practice, especially with pet care professionals, the first step for a person to manage compassion fatigue is to recognize what losses they have previously experienced. When an individual discovers personal ways to effectively heal their past grief, their emotional and physical health increases.

To be honest with you, before you can truly help someone grieving, you must work through you own issues concerning grief, loss, and dying. Helping people who are experiencing the loss of a pet can be draining. If you do not take precautions, burnout is a very real possibility.

Oftentimes the first sign that a person is not dealing with past losses is compassion fatigue. I have experienced many pet care professionals that are depleted of their emotional resources. When they do discover they have some unresolved grief about a particular loss, they begin to realize why it is so difficult to come to terms with their current grief. This is particularly true with caregiving professions.

I have also found that many people, including pet care professionals, find loss as something they would like to avoid totally, or even more detrimental—they believe they don't have any feelings of grief anymore from past loss experiences.

When this is the case, a new experience can easily trigger the memory of a past loss and unaddressed feelings once again resurface years later at inconvenient moments and in unwelcomed ways. Every loss is important, and it is part of life and cannot be avoided. Losses are necessary for growth, which is also part of life. When we grieve and accept loss, our life can take on a deeper and richer meaning. You will be healthier, more balanced, and ready to handle difficult grief situations.

I am not saying here that loss is easy or fair, but it is part of life. And as a pet care professional who is a valuable part of a pet's team—dealing with your own losses is crucial. It will make you that much more effective at providing care to your patients.

Common Losses in a Person's Life

Before I share ways that I help my pet care professional clients understand their own relationship to loss, I would like to share with you a brief list of some of the most common losses other than pet loss:

- Moving to a new neighborhood, state, or home, and leaving friends behind

- A best friend moves

- Relationship breakup

- Losing or changing a job

- Leaving home

- Divorce and separation

- Death of a close friend or family member

- Being rejected

- Changes in friendship

- Loss of a physical ability

- Loss of financial security

- Chronic illness

- Graduation from school

- Fire or theft

This is not by any means a comprehensive list of losses, but it will get you thinking on how to answer some of the questions that I am going to ask, so you can better understand your experience of loss in life. First, let's see how Jennifer, a veterinarian receptionist, discovered her unresolved grief.

Jennifer, Veterinarian Receptionist and Certified End-of-Life and Pet Loss Grief Mentor

Jennifer started working with me because I was consulting with her boss and office staff on how their practice could become more effective with helping their clients.

One of the first places to start the chain of support is sometimes with the receptionist as they are the ones that get that first phone call from a distressed human client.

Jennifer decided with the support from her boss that she wanted to take her studies further and become a certified end-of-life and pet loss grief mentor. We worked together, and she graduated as one of my star pupils.

I urge that as you read about Jennifer's experience uncovering her former grief experiences, you also think about your own. It doesn't matter what type of pet care professional you are—you will experience the same questions as Jennifer did.

Keep in mind, these are NOT questions to ask clients. These are for you to become aware of past grief that may be affecting your health, attitude, and tendencies as a pet care professional. These questions are only a small sample of what Jennifer explored, but they are enough to get you started with your own journey.

Jennifer Begins Her Journey

The first question that I had Jennifer explore was "Can you reflect on one of the earliest significant losses in your life?"

I recommend that you begin here as well. It can help you explore a pattern with other losses in your life. It is a way for you to take a loss inventory.

Review them yourself or with an end-of-life coach as Jennifer did with me. Allow yourself to reflect on how your past losses are influencing you right now.

As you discover what your earliest and most significant loss was, ask yourself these questions as well:

- How did it happen?

- How old were you?

- Where did it take place?

- What actually happened?

- Who was involved?

Other Questions to Consider

Once you have a clear understanding of that unresolved grief experience, begin to ask the next questions:

- What feelings of grief did you experience during that time?

- Did you have any reactions to the loss and what were they?

- Did anyone give you suggestions or advice on how to handle the loss?

- Were there any lessons that you learned from this early loss experience?

- Were there any myths that may have hindered the way you cope today?

- What did you learn about loss at an early age that helps you today?

Jennifer had a bit of difficulty with these questions and told me, "Wendy, I don't know if I can answer these questions. They are really difficult for me. Now that I know about my past unresolved grief—the feelings are scary."

I guided Jennifer to take her time because there is no timetable. I stressed how important it was for her to deal with these feelings, so she could become a better receptionist and mentor for others.

After you explore these questions, continue with the next two questions when you think about a recent loss and how you are coping:

- How did your early experiences with loss affect the way you respond to your most recent loss?

- When you think about that early loss now, are there things you wish were different?

Here is how Jennifer answered these questions:

Question 1: How did your early experiences with loss affect the way you respond to your most recent loss?

Answer: "I found in my 20 years of being a veterinarian receptionist I developed so many bonds with so many different animals and people. I had many favorites, and when they died, I was at a loss for words and said some pretty silly things that I thought were helpful. I realized many of these things I was saying were what my parents had told me. They shared ridiculous ideas about death, like when I was eight and my dog Patches died, my parents told me Patches went to a farm. I realize how much I stuffed my feelings in with each of my own pets after that. Once I discovered this, I realized I no longer felt uncomfortable listening to a grieving pet owner."

Question 2: When you think about that early loss now, are there things you wish were different?

Answer: "When I think about that early loss now, when Patches died, I wish my parents had told me the truth. It is so important for children to know the truth and process that grief in order to become healthy adults."

In my book *Healing a Child's Pet Loss Grief: A Guide for Parents* one of the topics that I address is the importance of telling your children the truth and not creating myths surrounding death. Of course, different age groups perceive death differently, and your responses will reflect that. Being clear and informative with your responses will help them to develop a healthy attitude towards death just like Jennifer shared.

Next Step

After she explored all of her unresolved grief and answered the above questions as well as others, Jennifer did the next exercise. I encourage you to do the same after you discover your earliest experience of grief.

Take a look at the following statements and answer based on how you feel right now.

Answer the "Final Statements" below with one of the following:

- Rarely/Never

- Sometimes

- Often

- All the time

Final Statements

- I feel lonely.

- I feel incompetent.

- I find it easier to take care of others rather than myself.

- I find it difficult to ask for support from others.

- I find it difficult to express my feelings.

- I struggle with addictions or eating disorders.

- I have a negative outlook on life.

- I want to hurt myself.

- I feel like quitting my job.

- I feel like eating a box of cookies, etc.

- I don't feel like eating.

- I have anxiety.

- My clients are making me angry.

- I have no patience for my clients anymore.

- I don't want to talk to people.

When you answer these final statements, it will help you determine if you truly recognize your unresolved feelings of grief and loss. It gives you a baseline for how much you have grown and/or how much you still need to explore. It can also uncover why you may have some unresolved grief around a particular loss. Consider this exercise a helpful tool when setting your goals for managing compassion fatigue.

Concerning that exercise, Jennifer told me, "When you gave me this list of Final Statements, I was a little concerned that I had not fully uncovered my unresolved grief. But I was pleasantly surprised to see and feel how far I've grown. Our clients and even my boss told me I appear happier and more at ease. Who would have thought what happened to me when I was eight would affect me now? I am so grateful to have been able to uncover and process that lingering grief."

Chapter Wrap-Up

Pet care professionals are busy people. We want to help our clients first before we take care of ourselves. A key to taking care of yourself means identifying any losses that occurred in your life—even in your early childhood—that remain unresolved.

If you take time to identify any such early, unresolved losses, then you'll likely be able to see the ongoing ill effect they've had in your life. The next step is to process that unresolved grief. If you decide not to, then compassion fatigue may set in with burnout following close behind—both of which you want to avoid.

You learned how Jennifer processed her early experiences of unresolved loss by doing the self-exploratory exercises in this chapter. Take time to do those exercises, so you can make those same gains. Confronting and processing any unresolved losses in your early life will enable you to help your clients in a healthy and effective manner.

Use the three *Quick Reference Tips* at the end of the chapter to continue to take care of your wellness. And remember that even though this work is rewarding—grief can sneak up on you and cause great distress if you first don't take care of any unresolved grief you may have.

Chapter 7 Quick Reference Tips

1. Each time you encounter a grieving client, your own unresolved grief may also be triggered.

2. This triggering of your grief will force you to deal with early grief, loss, and death experiences. Until you process these experiences, you could be headed toward burnout and not even know it.

3. Understanding your earliest most significant loss first is the beginning of your road to self-discovery and to your giving informed and satisfying support to others who are grieving.

8. Taking Care of Yourself

As a pet care professional myself, who deals with illness and death every day, if I don't take care of myself, I'll burn out very quickly. Even though my work is rewarding—it's draining. I incorporate many self-care activities into my days and weeks. They are activities that I enjoy and look forward to, and in turn they lead to making me better able to help my clients. I don't always do the same self-care activity every day. Instead, I mix it up so that I am always engrossed and not at all bored.

As mentioned throughout this book—it is critical to take care of yourself first because in doing so, you are at your best to give your clients the best. Following this advice will keep you clear and levelheaded. When making your health a priority, it will provide the stamina you need to cope with daily stresses.

Taking care of yourself is not being selfish, as some of my clients who are also pet care professionals have expressed to me. They feel guilty for spending time in nature, getting massages, having fun, or relaxing periodically throughout their workdays. I love sharing with my clients that selfish is not a bad word if used for the betterment of our individual self in order to best position ourselves to better the world at large.

In this chapter you will learn ways to take care of your physical, mental, and spiritual health, starting with the story of Donna whom I coached.

Case Study—Donna, Wildlife Rehabilitator

Wendy, before I started working with you, I was a mess. I wasn't sleeping, I was eating way too much sugar, and I spent most of my time taking care of the animals in my care. In fact, there were many times I stayed up all night with injured animals.

My health was affected, and I was headed down the rabbit hole. Luckily my staff veterinarian heard about you and recommended I call you. When I learned how to delegate some duties, hire more people, and create me time—my personal and work life changed.

Yes, I am still totally dedicated to my work and the animals—I love what I do. But I no longer feel guilty when going out for a run, meditating when stressed, and making sure I always have healthy food choices. I know the best way I can help the animals is by taking care of myself first, as contradictory as that may sound!

Donna is not alone in her journey. I have experienced similar stories with many different types of pet care providers that are obviously burned out because self-care didn't exist.

Take Self-Care Seriously!

As pet care professionals, I believe we have an obligation to our clients to be and give the best we can. You can't do this if you are not managing your stress first. What better way is there to begin managing your stress than by taking care of yourself first?

Because pet care professionals tend to be empathic, it is easy to put your clients' needs ahead of your own. In this way you can lose sight of a personal self-care program and feel as if you don't have the time. One of the biggest favors you can do for patients, clients, colleagues, staff, and family is to take self-care and stress control seriously.

As you know, working in the pet care industry has many rewards. Namely, you get to meet some amazing animals and wonderful people. Another reward involves assisting your human clients, so they feel supported as they journey through their grief.

This involvement is difficult to engage in if you are not managing those difficult feelings that accompany dealing daily with euthanasia, chronic illness, or the occasional death of a favorite animal client (chapters 7 and 9). And, of course, not having a daily outlet to manage these feelings only exacerbates the difficulty. When you do have a self-care protocol, the quality of your business will be better.

While all of my professional clients often express they feel guilty for taking time for themselves, everyone needs to know that it is totally okay to do this. Not only is it okay, it is necessary. Self-care is actually a great way to manage your pet grief to allow greater focus, productivity, and compassion in your business relationships.

Best Advice to Avoid Burnout

The best advice that I can give you right now and that I gave to Donna—carve out time every single day to replenish your own body, mind, and soul. It's necessary and important.

If you are tired, burned out, stressed out, not eating or overeating, and not sleeping because you feel the need to take care of your patients and clients 24/7, then I can assure you, you will grow tired of what you are doing. You will become less and less effective at it too.

This is the time to take care of yourself so that you are functioning as best you can and not relying on your reserve.

As Donna discovered, having strength is critical to being ready for unexpected feelings of grief, emergencies, dealing with clients, and the challenging medical decisions you might contend with every day.

Basics of Self-Care

There are many things that you can do for yourself that are easy, quick, and effective. Some of my "fast favorites" are:

- taking a moment to breathe before I talk to a client,

- visualizing a peaceful nature scene,

- reading an inspirational quote or poem,

- looking at a picture of a loved one,

- catching a quick power nap, and

- throwing a ball for my dog, Addie.

The longer versions for my self-care include participating in competitive ballroom dancing, walking in nature, meditating, taking a nap, taking a bath, hanging out with friends, listening to relaxing music, getting a massage, turning off my computer, or having a cup of tea.

I advise you to create a self-care plan that you know you can do. The important thing is to create success for yourself and choose activities that make sense and are attainable.

The healthier you are in body, mind, and spirit, the easier it is to cope and deal with compassion fatigue and avoid burnout.

Physical Health

When you do one or more of the following physical things for your body, you will feel stronger and more in control of your grief. Even if you can do something for only five to ten minutes a day, it still helps you on your journey.

I suggest that you spend at least a half-hour every day, if you can, with any combination of the following activities for the health of your body:

- Find a massage therapist for different types of massage modalities.

- Take a quiet walk in nature and listen to her sounds.

- Try energy bodywork like Reiki or Integrative Manual Therapy.

- Find an exercise class that suits you.

- Be sure to eat healthy foods throughout the day.

- Make sure you get enough sleep to regenerate.

- Take short breaks throughout the day with your eyes closed.

- Take notice to breathe intentionally and actively, even for just 3 breaths.

- Walk around your office building for short breaks.

- Eat lunch outside.

If a half-hour every day is too much time, try to give yourself a half-hour at least three times a week to take care of your physical body or when you find that you are experiencing anxiety or stress.

Mental Health

The next thing to take care of is your mind. It is easy for a pet care professional to get wrapped up in a client's grief. Your client could be in such a state of anxiety and stress that in being an empathic provider, you can take on their emotions without even knowing it.

To help your mind be healthy, there are many things that you can do for yourself. Finding the right ways to support your mind's health can take some time, but if you know what you are looking for, the process can be less stressful.

Here are some of the ways that you can create a healthy mind that can support you and keep burnout at bay:

- *Be real and go there*—this can be a difficult thing to do for people-pleasing professionals, but it is important to connect with your values and stick to them. True happiness and burnout prevention depend on this, so make the effort to do it.

- *Increase your positive statements.* One of the signs of burnout is the increase of negative emotions, statements, and feelings. Make it a point to notice the good things people do and stop being hard on yourself. When you add more positive statements and emotions to your daily self-talk, your resilience will increase.

- *Get support if you need it.* It takes time and effort to maintain healthy social connections. Supportive people are the best when you want to avoid burnout. Do not look for personal support from your clients; instead choose wisely and choose only those colleagues, friends, and family who do not judge you.

- *Have creative outlets.* When you burn out, you cannot do your job effectively. You might become increasingly rigid, less accurate, and less flexible, which will lead to your missing some important decisions. When you do something creative—like boat building, flower arranging, cake decorating, basket weaving, or harmonica playing—you will be more motivated to help your clients and less prone to feeling drained.

Choose a couple of these options that make sense to you. Burnout and compassion fatigue are complicated, but they both can be prevented. Self-care really is a must-do if you are dealing with pet loss occasionally or every day. Helping your clients deal with their grief and taking care of yourself is not exclusive of one another.

Spiritual Health

Now let's talk about your spiritual health. My pet care professional clients often forget to include this in their self-care routines. Also if you are uncomfortable with your spiritual beliefs or do not have any—please keep in mind the following activities are still helpful.

Whatever your spiritual choice, remember—it is your journey. I encourage you to only incorporate a spiritual practice into your daily life if you feel it works for you.

Here are some of the ways that you can create spiritual health in your life:

- *Take time to meditate.* While managing your practice and the daily tasks that come with a pet business, it is crucial to devote time to your inner self. Five to ten minutes of daily meditation will help you relax, free your mind, and foster a strong relationship with your core beliefs.

- *Try yoga, tai chi, qigong, and other forms of spiritual physical practice.* Spiritual activities like these can reduce emotional and physical stress on your mind. They can also help boost the immune system, lower blood pressure, and reduce anxiety, depression, fatigue, and insomnia.

- *Learn to trust your intuition.* I teach clients to learn to trust their gut feelings. When people gain this knowledge, their decisions become well thought-out, their confidence is heightened, any stress and anxiety gets managed, and, of course, burnout becomes avoidable.

- *Make the time to practice.* Practicing your spiritual belief, no matter what your belief is, daily, weekly, or periodically, can help you gain a strong sense of ease and grounding.

I have shared with you many ways to take care of yourself. It is totally up to you on how you would like to include one or many of the suggestions.

Creating a self-care program for yourself is equally as important as taking care of your patients and clients. Taking care of yourself is important because you want to have the physical energy and presence of mind to provide the best you can for all those you affect. It is difficult to do that if you are tired, hungry, stressed-out, suffering from body aches, and more.

Use the chapter's three *Quick Reference Tips* to take action on your own self-care. Even if the only thing you can do right now is simple breathing to create balance in your life, that's okay!

Chapter Wrap-Up

In this chapter, I shared ways that helped so many of my professional clients avoid burnout and compassion fatigue. I encouraged you to take some time for yourself without feeling guilty. Caring for yourself in terms of your body, mind, and spirit is foremost.

By allowing time in your schedule for self-care, you will be able to spend more quality time with your family, friends, colleagues, staff, and clients. You'll make better decisions and be ready for any of your unexpected grief, as well as clients'.

In the next chapter, we are going to explore exactly how you feel about death and dying. In order to truly engage with your clients and be end-of-life safe for yourself, it is important to know exactly how you feel about death. Not an easy quest, but necessary.

Chapter 8 Quick Reference Tips

1. Taking care of your physical, mental, and spiritual self will help you avoid the burnout that often can come when supporting others with their pet loss.

2. Scheduling time for something special every day will lead to a more productive and effective practice/business.

3. Be creative with how you take care of yourself. It must make sense to you. If it is not working, try something else.

9. Feelings about Death and Dying

In order to offer compassionate support to clients and manage your own personal and professional balance, it's important to know exactly how you feel about death and dying.

If you don't explore your own beliefs on this subject, you could find yourself colluding with the myths of pet loss (chapter 3) and trying to navigate with great difficulty what to say to your client in a chaotic situation (chapter 5). It can be difficult to maintain a healthy work and personal balance if you're not sure of your feelings and beliefs.

Especially, if you want to take this grief work further and become an end-of-life and pet loss grief coach, then it is essential you determine your beliefs about death and dying. Whether you choose this route or you want to be less involved yet compassionate—this is one of the first steps you must work through to maintain equilibrium.

As mentioned in chapter 8, it's extremely important to think through and act upon taking care of yourself first to avoid draining yourself. My intention is for you to be able to support yourself and your clients in a healthy way. By working through your own issues you will have a very long and rewarding career, if you so choose.

Initial Questions for Determining Your Stance on Death and Dying

Begin by asking yourself:

1. How does it make me feel knowing that I will die someday?

2. What emotions come to the surface?

3. What fears do I have?

4. Do I feel guilty for anything I have or have not done?

5. Do I have any regrets?

6. Am I concerned with how I will die?

7. Are there things I need to do before I die?

8. Is there anything that I need to say to someone before I die?

9. Am I concerned about what will happen to me after I die?

10. Am I interested in my afterlife?

There may be other questions that come to mind as you read over this list and by all means explore them. One of them that I did not include in this list but feel is extremely important is dealing with past losses, which we already covered in detail in chapter 7.

Case Study—Dr. Linda, Holistic Veterinarian

Dr. Linda contacted me when she decided she wanted to open a pet loss grief department in her holistic veterinarian practice. She had been a veterinarian for over twenty years, and her patients were often those who had terminal illnesses.

Because her practice was primarily focused on pet hospice, she saw the need to advance her own training as well as that of her office staff to become certified pet loss mentors. Her goal was to add pet loss grief support to her practice as a service.

Plus, Dr. Linda dealt with decision-making about euthanasia multiple times per day, and she was adamant about providing "good deaths" for her patients.

I found my experience with Dr. Linda and her office staff thoroughly delightful. They were motivated, compassionate, and dedicated to the animals. For the most part everyone had balance in their personal lives (chapter 8), but where they were lacking was how they felt about their own mortality.

We spent a couple of week's together working through the questions I shared with you. The transformation of Dr. Linda and her staff was noticeable, resulting in a changed outlook for many. The other benefit was that once they implemented this support service and everyone was certified, the general mood of the office changed.

Here is what Dr. Linda told me during our last check-in appointment:

Wendy, the first thing I have to share with you is how valuable it was to work with you. You understood what we wanted and created a program for us that worked.

With these questions about our stance on death and dying, we decided to address the questions as a group because we decided it would be helpful to support each other with their challenging nature. My staff, at first, was a little reluctant because some of them are very young, but once we saw how similar our feelings on death and dying were, we were able to bond deeper as a team.

The result is that our human clients noticed. They commented on our knowledge and ability to offer useful support. I can't thank you enough for changing our lives, and the life of my practice.

I also found that through performing daily euthanasia and getting clearer on my own mortality beliefs, I nurtured a new appreciation for human beings.

The bond my clients have with their animals is revealing—the raw, soul-wrenching tussles they have when deciding to choose euthanasia and the bleeding emotions that people experience during a pet's last moments. As I am able to be with my clients at these moments, I am reminded of the unconditional love we give our pets.

I never thought of this until I purposely explored my own emotions about death and dying.

Dr. Linda's story is powerful, and working with her was an opportunity for me to grow as well. You may not be a veterinarian or have to make choices like Dr. Linda does. But you may have a client that wants your advice as to what they should do for the betterment of their pet.

As you explore your answers to these questions, you will also be given the opportunity to reassess how you are living your life, taking care of yourself, and managing your business. I find that gaining cognizance of my beliefs about death and dying has been extremely valuable in my own practice.

My View

I have a very good handle on my beliefs about death and dying. I always have since I was a young child. I never have been afraid of it, and I understand (probably because I am a biologist) that all living things die.

This is not to say I don't experience grief or feel tremendous sadness when my animals or my animal clients die. I do! I have survived many heart-wrenching experiences, yet I keep going. Over the years I have made it my priority to explore and learn everything about how I relate to my viewpoints on death and dying.

I experience grief and death every day in my work. I pay attention to my self-care program (chapter 8). I am always aware of new stances when my clients share their stories and viewpoints with me. If there is something new that I must personally address after I listen to their concerns, I explore that.

The relieving of suffering and providing a peaceful way of leaving this earth is gratifying, whether it be euthanasia or pet loss grief support. I believe that providing a "good death" experience is a gift that keeps on giving.

I also believe that connecting energetically to a pet in the afterlife, for those who believe in this concept, is a healthy way to cope with grief. Many people find great solace for grief healing when they explore the metaphysical.

Your Turn

After you explore your feelings and belief systems around death you will have a new outlook on your life. There will be aspects of your life that you will want to change, and there will be those that you wish to keep.

I suggest writing your discoveries down on paper. Keep a list as you think of your questions and your answers. Jot down new discoveries as they filter into your experiences via a client or patient. Death and dying are valuable teaching experiences, and they can trigger not only your emotions (chapter 1) but your belief system as well.

I recommend if you have an office staff that you share this exercise with them and watch how it can contribute to a healthier work environment when you and your team are addressing end-of-life issues with human clients.

Ask yourself how you feel about the afterlife. Do you feel it doesn't exist or have you had experiences that make you think about it? How does this make you feel?

Chapter Wrap-Up

In this chapter we continued with recommendations and tools for you to manage stress. When you learn about how you honestly feel about death and dying, you will be able to actively listen to human clients with presence, knowledge, and compassion.

Understanding your feelings and beliefs surrounding the fact that everything must die will help you avoid draining yourself, becoming fatigued, or not being effective for clients.

When you understand your beliefs, you will stay healthy on physical, emotional, and spiritual levels.

Use the three *Quick Reference Tips* to continue to take care of your wellness. And remember that in doing this rewarding grief work, stress can still sneak up on you and cause turmoil if you don't take care of yourself first.

Chapter 9 Quick Reference Tips

1. Part of the self-care process for yourself is to know exactly how you feel about death and dying. When you do—you can provide a "good death" experience for your clients.

2. Exploring the afterlife can supply you with answers and offer you solace. Energy lives forever, and it can be felt, heard, seen, etc.

3. Death is not to be feared. If you talk about it—it doesn't mean you are inviting death into your life.

The Business of Grief
Section Three

If you want to connect with people who are in distress and great grief and scared, you need to do it in a certain way. I move kind of slow. I talk kind of slow. I let them know that I respect them.

—James Nachtwey

10. Incorporating Grief Support Coaching

We are now going to explore how you can incorporate pet loss grief support in your business. There are varying approaches in which you can add this service, and it takes some exploring to figure out which one is best for you. I will talk about the three most common ways in which I coach pet care professionals in determining the best approach for them.

There are many facets to this type of work, and it takes a special person to maintain a solid life-and-work balance when grief support is part of their working life. Working with the grieving is not for everyone. The healthiest way to do this work is by clearly knowing both how you feel about death and dying, and how you approach managing your compassion and empathy.

In reading this book you now know the basic background of grief and its components (section 1). You learned how to take care of yourself, so you can offer the most to clients, manage potential compassion fatigue, and hopefully avoid burnout (section 2). Section 3 will help you decide how you want to proceed as a business owner in regard to offering grief support—if at all.

When choosing to incorporate pet loss grief support into your business, there are many important factors and questions to consider before you do so. When you have a solid understanding of your positions based on the important factors and questions, you are ready to make a decision.

If your decision is well considered and deliberated with clarity, the rewards are endless, and your longevity in your profession and offering of grief support will be strong. However, if you choose to do this work without training or on a whim, it will become very difficult to sustain. You also risk hurting someone.

Keep in mind that as a business owner, you do not have to do the grief support for your human clients yourself. You can outsource it or just choose to be well educated and able to offer a compassionate act of kindness.

Is It Right for Your Business?

I have many veterinarians, kennel owners, trainers, groomers, animal communicators, professional pet sitters, etc., who ask me, "How do I know if this is something I want to build into my business?"

Truly that is your decision, and I can't answer it for you. But what I can do is help you discover how much or how little you want to incorporate it into your existing business model.

Before you go ahead with answering the next set of questions, please refer back to chapter 9 where we discussed the importance of knowing your own personal feelings about death and dying. By revisiting that chapter as well as others in section 2, you will gain a deeper understanding of the subjects you'll likely be deliberating with clients about as a grief support coach, and your own responses to the questions will be very useful to making a decision about offering grief support coaching.

Initial Essential Questions

To determine whether you want to offer grief support to your human clients, I recommend you begin by thinking about the following questions:

- How comfortable are you surrounding death issues?

- Do you see death as something negative to be feared?

- How skilled of a listener are you?

- How comfortable are you with interacting with people who are experiencing a lot of emotions?

- Do you want to become a certified end-of-life and pet loss grief coach, or have one of your employees take this on?

- Would you rather just know the general background of grief and loss to be more effective with self-management and the compassion needed towards your clients?

- How much time are you willing to devote to this? And is there time for you to devote to it?

- What are your present and future goals in regard to this topic?

- How busy are you with your daily tasks, and is there time to add a dedicated service?

- Do you have the stamina to listen to grief, death, and dying stories every day or even at all?

- Why would you consider adding pet loss grief support to your business? Is it because it's your life's mission, for the additional income, or due to a desire to honestly help?

- Do you have the personality to offer grief support?

I recommend that with each question you take your time to come up with a solid answer. Keep in mind that whatever you decide, the overriding aim remains the same: first you must do the best you can for yourself, and from there you take care of your clients. As we've already determined: prioritizing in this way leads to your avoiding undue stress, fatigue, and ultimately burnout.

When you understand how to support grieving clients with information, tools, and guidance within your scope of knowledge, your love for your work will become deeply rewarding. In my opinion, helping people through their grief journey is an honorary service to humanity and nature.

The Next Essential Considerations

After you explore the above questions, the next step to figure out is how you would like to proceed with grief support implementation. There are many ways in which you can add grief services into your business. In my coaching program I help pet care professionals develop their own unique support services. The three most common ways in which to offer pet loss grief support are:

1. As a focused service in your practice that clients can pay for

Emily, the veterinarian technician in chapter 1, decided after about a year since we'd been working together to train to become a pet loss grief coach. Her boss liked the idea when she presented it to her.

Because their office performed euthanasia multiple times daily, this was a perfect fit for the practice where Emily worked.

Her boss told me, "Since we added this service, my practice now gives our clients the support they need. I feel great about it because I believe we are now providing a much-needed service for clients. Prior to implementing this I always felt as if something was missing."

2. As a resource to outsource to a trained individual

Denise, a professional dog walker in New York City, decided what was best for her was not to study to become a certified pet loss grief coach after working through her own grief concerns. Instead, she would offer grieving clients referrals to trusted pet grief experts.

In one month's time Denise had lost five dogs. It was a tough journey for her as each dog had started with her in her first month of business.

Denise shared with me, "At first I really wanted to become a pet loss grief coach and offer this service on my website. But after exploring my own feelings about death and dying, I realized it wasn't for me. Instead, I networked in my area and compiled a list of therapists and coaches. However, everything I learned from you when I was learning about my own relationship with grief gave me the tools to be a great listener and offer supportive comments to my clients."

3. As an informal offering on your part of caring yet educated support through simple comments and actions

This is what Denise did, and coupled with becoming knowledgeable about trained professionals that she could recommend, she made the appropriate choice for herself. She learned to not collude with death and grief myths (chapter 3) and became a master of offering extremely supportive comments to her clients (chapter 5):

> *I loved exploring the different ways that I could say supportive and compassionate words of wisdom to my clients. One thing I started doing was I would take a picture of their dog on one of our walking adventures. I made sure I captured something special. Then I added words of condolence to the picture. I bought beautiful frames to put the photo in and gave this as a gift to show my clients how much I loved their dog too. Each one was different and unique.*

All of these choices will depend on how much time you want to devote to your own education on grief. Of course, you can incorporate any combination of these three choices, and many do. It comes down to exploring your answers from those initial ten essential questions, deciding what you are willing to commit to, and committing to doing the work it takes to sustain your practice and/or approach.

In chapter 11 you will learn about the difference between a coach and a therapist in more detail. While coaches and therapists share a common objective for a client's health and well-being, they differ in their training, methods, and goals.

Chapter Wrap-Up

In this chapter you learned about possibilities for incorporating pet loss grief support into your practice and business. I offered ten initial essential questions for you to explore to help you decide if you have the stamina, desire, and love for the work.

It takes a special person to maintain the work-life balance that grief support work requires. Working with the grieving can be emotionally exhausting and can easily trigger your own grief and feelings about death and dying. It is critical to thoughtfully manage your compassion involvement.

This chapter will begin to help you decide how you want to integrate pet loss grief support into your business—if at all.

Use the three *Quick Reference Tips* to continue your journey in learning about pet loss support for your business.

Chapter 10 Quick Reference Tips

1. Consider how necessary pet loss grief support within your business is. Is this service a good fit for you, your clients, and your business?

2. It takes a special person to work with the grieving—it is not for everyone.

3. Actively listening to illness, death, and dying stories every day takes stamina and balance.

11. Coaching vs. Counseling

As we continue exploring the role of pet loss grief support in your practice or pet business, the next phase is learning about the difference between coaching and counseling.

As a certified end-of-life and pet loss grief coach, I get this question a lot—what's the difference between what you do versus what a therapist does?

While coaches and therapists share the objective to support a client's wellness and growth—coaches and therapists differ in their training, methods, and goals. Once you have this information you will be more effective in choosing the method that's right for you, the method that matches your clients' needs, and the method that will keep you far from burnout.

The first step in understanding the difference between coaching and therapy is the following:

- Seeing a psychologist or psychiatrist is an unquestionably good idea for someone who has reached the point of abnormal grief (chapter 1) or who is dealing with past end-of-life issues they have yet to resolve (chapter 7). For a person in such a place, a grief therapist, preferably who is also trained in pet loss, is the best option (over a coach).

- In the following descriptions I am not discounting the approach or effectiveness of a therapist. Their role is important. My aim is simply to highlight how exactly the way of thinking of a therapist is different from that of an end-of-life coach.

Please keep both of the above in mind as we continue our learning about the difference between grief support coaching and counseling.

A helpful way of gaining a general picture of how coaching and counseling differ is to hear how a person who has experienced both compares them. Let's do that.

Case Study—Daniel, a Client That Experienced Both Coaching and Counseling

Daniel called me after eight weeks of going to a licensed therapist. Although he had wonderful support from the therapist, he was feeling like he wasn't getting anywhere with his journey. That's why he called me. When we first spoke, this is what he told me:

> *Wendy, my therapist really helped me a lot to understand that my grief feelings are normal after I learned that my cat, Mergie, had cancer and I had to euthanize her. But what was frustrating was that after I stopped feeling better, I noticed that all my therapist seemed to want to do was fix me. He even said during my sixth appointment with him that I should be thinking about ways to get over Mergie and think about getting another cat!*

Daniel and I worked together for approximately eight weeks. His therapist gave him a good foundation for expressing his grief. We were able to immediately build on that foundation. I shared with him the information about the stages of grief (chapter 2), destructive myths related to grief (chapter 3), and options for reacting in a healthy way when someone says something unsupportive (chapter 5).

Together we also developed a plan in regard to his goals to get the support he needed. After the fifth appointment this is what Daniel shared with me:

> *I never realized how useful working with a coach could be. I felt totally in control, and your guidance kept me focused on my own journey. I got to do the work necessary to heal from my pain and never once did I feel like you wanted to fix me or rush my journey.*

Comparison of Education

The biggest difference between a coach and a therapist is the educational requirements of each.

Depending on the state in which you live, the licensing can vary for therapists. Licensed therapists have advanced education from a university in human development, family systems, ethics, research, and therapeutic methods. They are also required to have many hours of practical training that is supervised by a seasoned therapist.

Many therapists also have training in specific mental health issues, such as depression, anxiety, substance abuse, etc.

However, a life coach or end-of-life coach is not mandated to have any formal training or education for coaching at all. Anyone can call themselves a life or end-of-life coach. I have seen this so many times in my work. The training varies from none to weekend training to more rigorous and structured training.

Be sure you get support from a certified life or end-of-life coach, and one that is properly trained.

There are various forms of education and certification for coach training, so if you are thinking about becoming a coach, be sure you have training and preferably a certification in end-of-life and grief coaching from a respected program.

Training in various coaching programs is varied, and in my research the two most reputable programs for general life coaching are the International Coaching Federation and Fowler International Academy of Coaching.

Both of these organizations have set the standards in coaching. If you are looking for specialized training in end-of-life and pet loss grief, ask the instructor the following questions:

1. Which program did you graduate from?

2. Where did you get your end-of-life and pet loss grief training?

3. Can you describe that particular program in some detail and share any related documentation?

To be called "certified" in any type of coaching program requires individual study, case histories, and detailed documentation of each learning module. Not just a weekend seminar.

In general grief training and pet loss grief training are not much different. Grief is grief. However, in my opinion, it is more beneficial to refer clients to a therapist or coach that has education and a focus on pet loss needs, which oftentimes is a more rigorous training than that of other forms of loss.

Comparison of Objectives

A therapist's approach to pet loss grief is to help the client get over their grief while analyzing their process and progress. Therapists diagnose their clients. It is understood by therapists that for people to make significant changes in their lives, they must resolve their grief emotions (chapter 1) in order to take the necessary action to get back to normal.

End-of-life and grief coaching is primarily about helping people discover and achieve their goals, goals that the client and coach determine together at the outset of their work. Coaches, for the most part, work with clients that are coping with normal grief feelings rather than abnormal grief.

A grief coach will encourage clients to embrace their emotions, and they listen to what their clients are experiencing without analyzing the process or progress.

Their work focuses on creating and maintaining motivation and creating plans for change. A coach will walk the journey of pet loss grief with their client and empower their clients to make the best decisions. A coach never diagnoses a client.

Comparison of Ethics and Boundaries

There is a vast difference in ethics and boundaries between coaches and therapists. As a certified coach I find it disheartening that coaches don't have distinct and rigorous ethical standards. And I believe the issue lies with the fact that there is no licensing for coaches, so anyone can call themselves a coach.

When I was in coach training, it was expected of me to learn appropriate boundaries and follow a strict code of ethics in my practice. Yet, I find many pet loss grief support people do not have any guidelines whatsoever.

Therapists are legally required to maintain very strict ethical guidelines, confidentiality, and professional boundaries. However, because there is no legal regulation of life or end-of-life coaches, ethical standards are variable.

In my professional opinion this is the biggest issue: untrained people working as coaches with grieving pet owners. The lack of education, ethics, and boundaries in coaching can hurt vulnerable people. It is imperative that anyone helping people with pet loss grief issues be properly trained as a therapist or be certified as an end-of-life and pet loss grief coach by a reputable program.

Comparison of Approach

Because I love the coach approach when it comes to supporting people with pet loss issues, you may think that I am against therapy. To be clear, I think traditional therapy is extremely important and necessary, and I often recommend my clients to see licensed therapists.

Many people, however, find that when dealing with pet loss, conventional therapy has not worked for them in the long term.

Depending on the type of therapy, many of my clients have expressed that when working with a therapist, they just talked about their past issues of grief and loss without it relating to what they were experiencing in their present.

My clients' frustration is that they did not get helpful guidance for coping with their immediate loss. It's a lot of talk about past issues.

That is why so many of my clients love working with me as their coach. A coach is a partner who will offer actual guidance and ideas on how to reach a client's goals and handle a client's current reality. Coaches help brainstorm solutions and strategies for a client's current changing issues on their grief journey.

Both an ethical coach and therapist will always be sure that the solutions discovered are in line with a client's belief system, circumstances, and personality.

Working with a coach typically includes homework. The sessions typically offer the client a clear roadmap for change, as well as supportive guidance if the client is ready to make the change.

The Need for Pet Loss Grief Coaches

As a pet loss grief specialist I coach grieving pet people and guide them to bring out their personal (and professional) best in their unique journey. I don't fix or solve problems. The pet loss grief coach is there to gently help people discover and develop—on their own—what they need to heal.

I guide each client based on the inherent skills and talents they already have to achieve their goals. In most cases, my clients do have everything they need to heal their loss and deal with the inevitable end-of-life issues. For the most part, in the face of grief, compassion fatigue, or burnout, clients feel at a loss on how to recognize their own resources, especially when grief (or compassion fatigue and burnout) is new, unexpected, or triggered from unresolved losses (chapter 7).

As already mentioned in chapter 9, because people are typically afraid of death and don't want to talk about dying, many feel embarrassed, bewildered, or inadequate because they believe that their grief feelings are not "normal" (chapter 1).

When a person is experiencing this, it is important for them to have an end-of-life coach or a pet care professional that will get what they are going through.

A certified end-of-life and pet loss grief coach will partner with the person on their grieving, end-of-life, and mourning journey. This partnership is entirely client-focused and is built on a safe and trusting relationship.

In my Certified Pet Loss Grief Mentor program, I teach my students not to fix their clients. A licensed psychologist works in a different manner from this, with different goals than those of a coach.

A pet loss grief coach will walk alongside their coachee, listen intently, and ask powerful questions. This protocol will help the coachee to embrace what is currently happening to them internally. It will also help them understand what is happening to them by understanding why family, friends, coworkers, etc., may not understand what they are going through (section 1).

As a whole it is difficult to support ourselves when grief is raw. You may find a client or yourself experiencing feelings and emotions that make you feel as if you are going crazy. A coach will remind you that you are, in fact, normal and experiencing normal grief.

A coach will also help people not feel alone but supported. When loss stories need to be told, we need someone to listen. When our clients feel hopeless, a coach helps them form a new vision for the future and offers clients support as they establish a new normal (chapter 6).

Chapter Wrap-Up

When talking about the business of grief, you must address whether you want to add coaching or counseling to your practice. It really depends on your goals for your business.

Keep in mind that you can employ someone in this area, make referrals to outside experts in this area, or receive appropriate training yourself to offer this service in your business. I highly recommend not offering a grief service without the proper training.

You also heard from a client of mine who experienced both therapy and coaching. Daniel experienced benefits from both—but it was coaching that gave Daniel control over his journey.

In my experience seeking a coach over a therapist has been the choice for most of my pet care professionals when coping with compassion fatigue and burnout. Some have loved the coach approach so much they later became certified pet loss grief coaches themselves (chapter 10).

There are many things to consider when exploring coaching vs. therapy. With knowledge about coaches' and therapists' education, objectives, ethics and boundaries, and approaches you will be able to recommend the appropriate professional to clients.

In the next chapter, you will learn about the building blocks of coaching that I use in my practice. Knowledge of these building blocks is useful for any pet care professional that would like to support their clients. Keep in mind I am sharing these building blocks with you so that you can experience firsthand the high level of commitment certified coaches have for their clients.

Use the following three *Quick Reference Tips* to continue your journey in learning about the business of pet loss support.

Chapter 11 Quick Reference Tips

1. A therapist is appropriate for unresolved or abnormal pet loss grief issues. Whereas, a coach is the choice when someone is dealing with typical pet loss grief.

2. A coach will walk the journey of grief and death with their client so that the client will discover and become empowered by their experiences.

3. Coaches do not analyze, give solutions, fix, or help someone get over their pet loss. Coaches listen, guide, and celebrate the discoveries of their clients.

12. Building Blocks of Coaching

Some foundational principles of coaching that I use in my practice are what I call the eight building blocks of support. I utilize these principles whether I am working with a pet care professional suffering from compassion fatigue, a client who is deep in grief, or a student expressing their own beliefs around death and dying.

At the base of the grief-coaching building blocks is listening. When working with a client, you first listen to the story your client has to tell. A grief coach does not step in to monitor, direct, or prescribe a mourning protocol. A grief coach stays on the sidelines, listens, and offers to walk the journey with the client by applying the following eight building blocks of support.

Do you remember Dr. Steven from chapter 5 and how his staff was saying well-intentioned but unsupportive things to clients? When I presented these eight building blocks of support to them, they began to understand that the best support for clients was actively listening, not offering advice, and not trying to fix the person's pain.

Dr. Steven told me, "Wow, I always thought we were a supportive office. Yet when I learned these building blocks and encouraged my staff to learn them, plus we keep "cheat sheets" at our desks and in examining rooms as helpful reminders, after that, the stress went way down, both for staff and clients. Our clients even expressed they were thankful for our support. They told us they honestly felt like we cared."

Eight Building Blocks of Support for Pet Loss Grief Coaching

1. Offer a Safe Place

As mentioned in chapter 9, our society and culture have a difficult time with grief and death. Most of us are uncomfortable even being around a person who is experiencing the loss of an animal companion. Because you may be uncomfortable—you probably don't know how to respond (chapter 5).

I have had many a client tell me heart-wrenching stories about not getting the safe support they needed from pet care professionals, friends, or family members. They felt pushed by these others to let go of or get over the grief of losing their pet. They felt judged at every stage of their grief (chapter 2) and judged about their personal experience of mourning.

The result—people experiencing pet loss grief do not feel understood or supported. They literally feel "unsafe" in their environment to openly mourn their loss in their own way.

Since coaching is all about the grieving client, it is important to let them set the agenda and intensity. This will help the client feel safe.

Here are some ways that I offer my clients to create a supportive and safe place for them to grieve. I go into each of these in more detail in my training programs, but this is a great list to get you started. Here's the list:

- Allow them to hurt.

- Allow them to cry.

- Allow them to feel whatever they feel.

- Allow them to say what they want to say.

- Allow them to do whatever they want to do.

- Don't try to fix them.

- Don't judge what they tell you.

2. Ride the Roller Coaster with Them

When people experience grief, there are ups and downs on the journey. There are times of great heights, followed by periods of deep drops in emotions. These ups and downs can be unexpected with lots of turns, corners, stops, and goes.

When a person experiences their own grief with awareness, it is literally like getting on a roller coaster and hanging on for a breathtaking ride. To keep a coachee feeling safe there is a need for someone to get on that ride with them.

This is not to say they need someone to give them instructions on how to take their ride or correct them as to how to ride differently or better—they, instead, need a coach to be with them on the roller coaster ride, simply so they don't feel alone.

Here is a list to get you started with how to effectively ride the roller coaster with your client. Keeping this brief list in mind as your client tells their story will help you not only be end-of-life safe but also able to listen to your client compassionately.

- Before working with a client, walk through you own grief issues, so you can be present for that client (section 2).

- Don't say, "I understand," "I know what you are feeling," or "I went through the same thing." Those statements are diminishing.

- Avoid starting a statement with "At least . . . " Again, that's diminishing.

- Avoid attempts to change the pain. Remember, you aren't there to fix anyone.

- Avoid statements that begin with "You should . . . " or "You will . . ."

- Don't place a timetable on their recovery.

3. Let Your Client Tell Their Story

When a person is grieving, they need to tell their story—uninterrupted. When we give a safe place for someone to share what happened, this begins the necessary component towards their healing.

Telling a story is part of the mourning process. It is a way for a person to acknowledge the reality of the loss of their pet. It also creates a path to greet their pain and emotions. At the same time it offers an important way for them to hold onto memories and fond moments.

Storytelling is a soul-healing step towards finding the new normal (chapters 1 and 6).

The sad thing is there are not many people who will listen. It takes patience to listen to a client's story, so be prepared if you want to become a pet loss grief coach. It is about the grieving and their need to share. The same story will be told many times.

The grieving person needs to tell their story many times as it is a key way for them to process and accept the chronic illness or death of a beloved companion.

Here are some things that will be included in your client's stories:

- Memories

- Details about the relationship they had with their pet

- Details about the illness, tragedy, and what led up to their pet's death

- Emotions

- Uncertainties and struggles

4. Support Them with What Is Normal

In my coaching practice I have taken many a roller coaster ride and the most common question I get asked is "Am I going crazy?" The second question is "Am I normal?"

Since grief is unpredictable and can feel like a person is living on another planet, it can easily make a person feel as if what they are going through is weird, different, scary, and panic inducing.

One of the greatest things a coach can offer clients is helping them discover that what they are experiencing is normal (section 1).

However, there may be a time when grief is not normal, so the coach must be trained to recognize this in their client and refer them to the appropriate health care provider.

The International Coaching Federation has "Ten Indicators to Refer a Client to a Mental Health Professional." In my coaching program we go over these in great detail. This list will help you recognize what may be going on with your client, so you can make the appropriate referrals.

10 Indicators to Refer a Client to a Mental Health Professional

When your client is "significantly"—

1. exhibiting a decline in their ability to experience pleasure and/or exhibiting a significant increase in being sad, hopeless, and helpless.

2. having intrusive thoughts or the inability to concentrate or focus.

3. experiencing sleep issues, either in terms of a great difficulty getting to sleep, sleeping through the night, or excessive sleep.

4. experiencing a change in appetite, either a notable decrease or increase.

5. feeling guilty because others have suffered or died.

6. feeling hyper-alert or excessively tired.

7. experiencing increased irritability or outbursts of anger.

8. expressing intense feelings of despair or hopelessness.

9. displaying impulsive and risk-taking behavior.

10. experiencing any thoughts of death and/or suicide.

5. Patience—Give Your Client the Time They Need

The journey of grief can never be rushed. It is necessary for the grief coach to recognize when their client wants to rush their experience and get on with life.

In my own experience working with people experiencing pet loss grief, I do find, for the most part, they aren't trying to rush their grief experience. Yet, when I worked with people experiencing the loss of a spouse, parent, or friend, the urge to move on quickly was greater.

It is important for the end-of-life coach to give their client all the time that they need. Grief is not a quick trip. It can be a very slow journey, which never completely ends. A devoted pet owner cannot forget the dog that they shared their soul with or the cat that provided endless escapades of joy, especially when those animal companions gave such unwavering unconditional love.

In fact, devoted pet owners don't want to forget and shouldn't be expected to forget. Yet, there can be family members, friends, and partners that expect the grieving person to "get over it" quickly and will not hesitate to share an inappropriate comment with hopes to get the grieving person to move on. As a coach, you are likely the only one who gives the grieving pet owner the time, space, ear, and patience that they need.

There is no set timetable for getting over grief. However, there are time periods when a person feels their grief at varying levels of difficulty. An end-of-life coach is aware of these levels.

6. Listen First. Then Guide

When you listen and learn with your client, you will get to know your coachee in a deep way. And by asking them powerful questions, you can guide them into discovering new awareness about how to move forward in their journey of pet loss grief.

If you take on the attitude to listen and learn, rather than approach your work as a teacher, your client will feel safe to express what they are going through. When you listen, the coachee will feel as if you are interested in what they have to say. It will enable them to feel safe, heard, and able to take charge of their own journey.

As your client trusts you and shares their journey with you, the better you can support them.

7. Help Them Discover Their New Normal

In chapter 6 we talked very specifically about the new normal. This is the time when a grieving person begins to recognize that their thoughts, decisions, and changes in regard to their life are different without their pet.

The first place to begin in helping someone discover their new normal is providing a safe place for that person to mourn. Pain needs to be felt, embraced, and accepted. Like many of the other stages of grief (chapter 2) there is no time limit. Everyone is different, every pet is different, and every unique experience will dictate the outcome.

Since coaching is about moving forward in life—finding a new normal involves forming a new vision for the future. It also includes designing goals, determining strategies, and identifying a support team.

I talked in detail in chapter 6 about the five common ways in which people find a new normal, but I will list them here for quick reference.

The 5 Common Ways to Find a New Normal

1. A new identity

2. A new relationship with the pet that died

3. A new group of friends

4. A new sense of purpose

5. A celebration of their growth

8. Celebrate Growth

As you know from reading this book, growth from experiencing grief takes on a life of it own, comes in many forms, and takes work. The outcome also depends on a person's outlook, perceptions, and choices.

Walking the journey of pet loss grief is challenging. No one really chooses to experience grief, but we all go through it. Some find it to be a challenging, difficult, and negative experience, but for many they eventually feel that their grief allowed for a deep and profound growth experience.

As a pet loss coach working with people all over the world, one of the greatest experiences I have had is to help clients realize their growth and then be able to celebrate this stage with them.

Dr. Steven shared with me, "Every month as part of grief maintenance, as a staff we do a life celebration of all the animals in our practice that we had to euthanize that month. We celebrate and share special lessons each of these animals gave us. This helps us tremendously to process our grief."

The critical part of this particular building block is to recognize when your client is ready to celebrate. Some questions to ask are:

- What have you learned from the loss of your beloved companion?

- How has your grief made you a better person?

- What did your loss teach you that you couldn't have learned in another way?

Some days will continue to be raw, difficult, and emotional. When someone is grieving, they need to be able to go back to their normal feelings of grief. Yet, as they move through the stages of grief, it is very meaningful to celebrate accomplishments.

Chapter Wrap-Up

A certified end-of-life and pet loss grief coach follows the eight given building blocks of support to ethically and effectively support their clients. At the foundation of grief support is listening: the coach first listens to their client's story and does not step in and do the work for their client.

In the next chapter, you are going to learn the importance of following up with clients. Following up periodically shows that you are available and giving clients the time and safe space to grieve. This little extra service that any pet care professional can do shows you remember each client and their companion too.

In your *Free Pet Loss Grief Resources Packet* you will also find a list of these eight building blocks of support. You can find that free resource at the beginning of this book and in the resources section, and then download it from there.

Use the three *Quick Reference Tips* to continue your journey in learning about the business of pet loss support.

Chapter 12 Quick Reference Tips

1. Safety is the most critical and important building block when building trust with a grieving person.

2. Listening, learning, and not being the expert with your client will help them heal their grief because someone is listening to them tell their story and riding the roller coaster of grief with them.

3. Know that it is okay to celebrate when a client discovers a powerful lesson from the grief of losing a pet. Timing for this is important, and it is on your client's terms.

13. Following Up with Compassion and Resources

One of the ultimate acts of kindness you can do for your clients—even if you choose not to incorporate pet loss support in your business—is to follow up with them. When you check in with them after the death of their pet and beyond, it shows a client you care.

This topic is important to discuss in regard to the business of pet loss support because it also tells them that their beloved companion meant something to you and that they are not alone with their pain.

However, timing and frequency are important. If you want to have a continued relationship with a client, knowing how and when to support them after the initial loss, then this chapter is useful.

Why You Should Reach Out

It's important for people that are grieving to know that someone understands and cares enough to reach out. Even to this day, when I get a card from our veterinarian, groomer, and pet sitter after one of my companions died—it means the world to me. What is even better is when one of them sends me a card on a holiday—in memorandum that celebrates the life of my animal that has died.

As a pet care professional, you can show your client that you get what they are going through by following up in a few simple ways. This gesture can go a long way towards building a relationship and continued referrals.

Even if they don't come to you for grief support or they don't need your services any longer because they no longer share their life with an animal—sending them a sympathy card will tell your client that you appreciate them and their loyalty in a very compassionate way. There are many other ways in which you can follow up as well, which I list below.

Compassionate Follow-Ups

- Call them on the phone and speak directly to them.

- Send flowers.

- Send a donation in their pet's name.

- Create a memorial wall/garden and ask for them to come in and add a photo/plant.

- Write a personal letter about what their pet meant to you.

- Send them a relevant quote in a beautiful frame.

- Give them a pet memorial stone, keychain, necklace, etc.

You may already be following up with them soon after their companion died with cards and/or gifts, and that is a great beginning. Knowing the right time to show your continued support is also important.

Before discussing timing in more detail, let's revisit Katharine, the dog groomer from chapter 4, to see how she paces her remembrances.

Case Study—Katharine, Dog Groomer

Do you remember Katharine, the dog groomer from chapter 4 and how she experienced the changing themes of her grief with Emma? And the fear she had about meeting Gracie, the new dog? And the uncomfortable feelings that she was experiencing with her own grief?

I am going to share what Katharine did for Emma's people at each milestone of their personal grief journey. Here's how Katharine explained it to me:

When I first decided I wanted to do more for my human clients than just send a sympathy card, I was a little overwhelmed on how to organize more follow-ups. So, I created a spreadsheet with all my animal clients that were still living and those that had died. I added the dates of their birthdays, deaths, holidays, and other personalized dates. It then became easy to implement follow-ups into my grooming business. I also kept a record of the special personality traits of my animal clients, so I could send appropriate gifts and cards. It's been fun, rewarding, and easy to implement.

Keep in mind, you don't need to be a coach or a therapist to offer follow-ups like this in your business. And, as Katharine attests, staying in touch with clients does go a long way. A welcomed outcome of Katharine's incorporating continued contact and follow-ups into her business was that she gained a huge referral list.

When to Acknowledge

During the First Year—General Background

The first year is the most difficult for people going through pet loss. A client will be adjusting to not having their beloved companion physically with them on a daily basis. This would be the period for you, as a pet care professional, to acknowledge the loss specifically at multiple times.

Your client will also be undergoing some "first-time experiences" throughout the year. The examples below are some that you can be aware of and acknowledge with a kind gesture or meaningful words when the client comes into your office, kennel, store, or shop.

These first-time experiences can trigger strong feelings of loss. It is almost as if the person experiences their pet dying all over again. The best you can do is be aware of these "firsts" and then offer the appropriate remembrances.

1. The first holiday without their pet to share in the festivities

2. The first time they experience walking alone if they shared that activity with their companion

3. The first time going to a special place they once shared with their companion without them

4. The first anniversary of the pet's death

The First Weeks . . . What You Can Offer

Within the first week or when you just hear the news—send a card or other gift. It is never too late to send a kind message in regard to loss. You can also send an email, e-card, or other form of virtual message. However, I have found that a card sent through the mail is more meaningful for the person experiencing grief.

Keep in mind the importance of the appropriate things to say if you choose to write a personal note or letter (chapter 5) and not to collude with the debilitating myths (chapter 3).

I always send a card with a handwritten letter as soon as I receive the news. If I had a special relationship with that animal, I send flowers or another appropriate gift.

During the first few weeks, grief is extremely raw, and the person will be vulnerable to changes in their environment and reactions from friends and pet care professionals.

For many it is a blur. For others, it is draining and painful. After a few weeks, the grieving person may begin to feel unsupported or alone. Grieving has just started, and they may reach out to you. Keep in mind, if they do, their grief can be demanding.

Not only is your client beginning to realize the physical loss of their companion, but also they may be re-experiencing some losses from the past (chapter 7), which could complicate their current grief. When you are aware of this, then act as a resource or a listening ear to help your client get through these weeks.

The tricky part is you must be aware of your available time and schedule. It is a delicate balance to show support to a client and not allow your business to suffer. Keep this aspect in mind as you decide how much you want to integrate pet loss grief into your business.

It is important to know your business' boundaries for you to stay healthy within this type of work. It is impossible for you or your office to be available 24/7. By deciding on a plan on how to deal with those clients that need a lot of time, pop in unexpectedly, or call numerous times, you and your staff will remain end-of-life safe.

However, when you do get these unexpected visits or phone calls, a few minutes of listening is helpful. In my certification course we explore this in detail.

If you find that your office or business cannot support the time needed to listen a referral is the appropriate next step. The key is for your clients to know you care and are a resource and then direct them to the appropriate support method.

I can guarantee those clients that trust you will be reaching out because they expect that you get what they are going through. Even if they don't reach out immediately, a brief, kind note or a small gift from you is very healing.

Three Months . . . What You Can Offer

Around this time I send out another card with a personal note stating that I am thinking of them. If you want to send an email, e-card or other virtual message you can. Keep in mind—no matter your delivery choice the theme for this remembrance is courage and patience.

The first three months is a difficult time for those who are experiencing grief and loss. I have seen in my practice grief emotions intensify during the journey. When this first happens with a client they can become afraid of their emotions. They may not understand why and what they are experiencing. They can also be confused and impatient that they are still feeling sad.

What happens during the first three months is that people begin to realize the reality of the death of their beloved companion is permanent. If you choose to send a remembrance during this time—send one that illuminates strength.

Katharine, the dog groomer, sends a homemade card with a picture of the pet on it and a personal note with one of her favorite quotes.

Here is what she wrote for Emma's people at the three-month anniversary of Emma's death:

> *Emma was a light in my life. Whenever she came to visit me, my heart would brighten up. I always loved seeing Emma's name in my schedule.*
>
> *I would like to share a quote that makes me think of Emma—*
>
> > *How lucky I am to have something that makes saying good-bye so hard.*
> >
> > —A.A. Milne

Remember, this can be a challenging time for you as well, especially if you had a special relationship with that particular pet.

The Anniversary of the Death . . . What You Can Offer

I don't know anyone in my practice that needs this reminder. It is one of the top "firsts" that I talked about in chapter 12.

In my experience, on this first anniversary there is usually a rush of pain that equals that of the actual day of their pet's end of life. There is also an uneasy anticipation of this anniversary. This is when I get the most calls because people are gearing up, knowing that this is going to be a challenging time for them.

Planning ahead is something I encourage my clients to do. Talking through their feelings around the anniversary is also healing. The anniversary on the whole can be an opportunity for more healing.

Here are some special acts your clients may choose to do to turn the potentially challenging anniversary into an uplifting milestone:

1. Honor their pet in a special way

2. Honor themselves on surviving the grief

3. Share stories and memories

4. Write a letter to their pet thanking them

I encourage my clients to spend this day as they wish and to know that I am there to support them.

Around this time I send out to my clients a photo of their pet in a frame and a beautifully designed list of things to do to celebrate the life they had with their pet.

Holidays and Special Days . . . What You Can Offer

Facing the holidays can also be an incredibly difficult time, especially if a person celebrated and did fun activities with their pet on birthdays, holidays, family gatherings, and wedding anniversaries (especially if the pet was present at the ceremony).

Just as with the anniversary of the death of their pet, during holidays, a client may become extremely aware of the void. It can be a very difficult time for them to be celebratory during these holidays if their pet usually was there with them.

The sights, sounds, and smells of a holiday may trigger the fond memories of their pet, and this alone will break their heart. A coach is paramount for guiding their coachee to prepare for these days.

As a pet care professional, you may or may not be faced with this in your business. If you are a kennel owner, pet sitter, or dog walker, you likely face clients in this position, especially if your client has multiple animals and they employ your services during holidays.

For them, showing up at your establishment may be one of the most difficult things to do. The best you can do when this happens is to support them within the scope of your training with end-of-life issues.

Katharine does something wonderful in her grooming shop on one particular holiday, National Pet Memorial Day, which falls on the second Sunday of September. Katharine takes one of the walls in her shop and invites clients to come in and post pictures of their deceased pets. She plays soft music and has candles burning throughout the day. Her clients love this.

I also work with a veterinarian practice that hosts an annual *Life Celebration Memorial Night*. They send cards inviting all their clients who lost a pet during the past year. They encourage the attendees to bring photographs of their pets to share.

This night is incredibly important for those who attend. Friendships are formed, and support is meaningful. This veterinarian practice recognizes the importance of taking care of their clients.

Resources for Your Clients

Before we end this chapter, it is important to share general ways to support your clients. Besides sending cards, flowers, or other gifts—there are many resources that you can offer. I will list some of the common ones to have on hand:

1. Know where the pet grief support groups are in your area and online. Be sure the people running these groups are certified and reputable grief coaches or therapists.

2. Have a list of pet loss hotlines available for clients.

3. Share some pet loss poems or pet loss quotes. I have several great ones on my website.

4. Have a list of emergency phone numbers to give your clients.

5. Supply a list of local and online coaches, psychologists, psychiatrists, and psychotherapists that specialize in grief.

6. Recommend clients to visit my website and download the free gift, so they can get support right away.

7. Compile a list of crematoriums, pet funeral homes, pet cemeteries, etc.

8. Have a pet loss grief library in your office. A list of my bestselling and award-winning books on pet loss grief can be found in the resource section of this book; please consider including them in your office library.

Chapter Wrap-Up

When someone loses a pet, their life can get fairly chaotic and difficult. Even though they may have some support, they will probably reach out to you, as their pet care professional, as well. This demonstrates that they trust you. When you express useful and well-thought-out condolences, it will deepen that trust because it illustrates you care and their pet was also special to you.

You learned how Katharine, the dog groomer, incorporated a rather detailed system for following up on special and critical occasions after the deaths of clients' pets. With her system in place, Katharine's business tripled because she became known for her compassion.

Timing and frequency are important to know when and how to support your clients.

Finally, having a list available of local and online resources related to pet loss grief is essential for you as a business owner. People that are grieving need to know that someone understands and cares enough to reach out and provide solutions and support.

Here are the final three *Quick Reference Tips* to help you with the choices that you make for your business. When you implement pet loss follow-up into your business, your human clients will appreciate your kindness and thoughtfulness.

Chapter 13 Quick Reference Tips

1. Following up with clients after the deaths of their pets shows that you care and are compassionate. It tells them you get what they are going through.

2. There are many "first-time" moments that your client will experience during the first year after their pet reaches the end of life. It is important for you to be aware of those "firsts" and to show sensitivity.

3. Having a list handy of local and online resources related to pet loss grief is a must.

Time to Join Forces

In our culture we are beginning to view pet loss grief, death, dying, and celebrating the life of our companions with much greater awareness and sensitivity. It is a wonderful trend. However, we still have a lot to learn and there is work to be done, which is why I wrote this book.

It is also why I am more than happy to offer a Certified Pet Loss Grief Mentor training to pet care professionals wanting to become end-of-life and pet loss grief coaches.

We live in a culture that generally doesn't deal well with illness, death, end-of-life events, and the process of grief and dying. We don't like to talk about death.

If the topic is brought up or someone dies, the subject is oftentimes changed or a person may even walk away to avoid it and all the feelings that come with it. Death and grief make people uncomfortable.

I have heard from countless people, "I am so afraid to talk about death and grief because I worry I'll make it worse!"

Because of this belief and others, we have come up with euphemisms that are related to death. Instead of saying a pet is dying or a pet has died, we say they "passed away," "transitioned," or "crossed the rainbow bridge." There are many more of these euphemisms, and the issue with them is they take us away from reality, prolong grief, and make it harder for people to engage with the necessary grief work. When a lack of engagement with grief work happens to pet care professionals, it typically leads to compassion fatigue, burnout, and careers getting cut short.

Part of my job as a certified end-of-life and pet loss grief coach is to help pet care professionals manage compassion fatigue and avoid burnout. This work is deeply rewarding because pet care professionals, for the most part, are caring and compassionate. Pet care professionals innately understand how to guide someone when they are hurting and will do so at the expense of their own health.

However, by having these qualities you, the pet care professional, also risk having to leave your life's work too soon because you didn't take care of yourself well (something I cover in detail in section 2). Feelings of sadness, anger, and anxiety left unattended can put you in the fast lane to compassion fatigue and burnout. When you create chaos in your personal and business life by not taking care of yourself and not attending to your emotional health, everyone is affected.

You have probably experienced various forms of pet loss grief. Maybe one of your favorite clients received news about their pet being terminally ill or dying suddenly and tragically. When clients shared their devastating news, it may have left you feeling inadequate because you didn't know how to help. The other issue is that you might have offered well-meaning but "too much" or "inappropriate" support. Saying the wrong thing or perpetuating a myth can create and trigger grief in anyone who is experiencing pet loss.

If you are in the veterinarian profession, you may struggle with delivering the news that an animal patient needs to be euthanized. There are kids involved, and the family is devastated. You may have cried in front of them, leaving you feeling embarrassed and unprofessional. Or they may have cried in front of you, and you didn't know the best way to handle it.

Holding back when expressing your sadness will wreak chaos on your psyche and well-being. It also does your client a disservice. I have had veterinarians ask how they can learn not to cry during euthanasia. Keep in mind, it is not unprofessional to cry. Families do want to know that you have a connection with their pet as well.

Managing your compassion fatigue and avoiding burnout come down to how you react to your stress. Certainly, dealing with death and dying is stressful, staff can become stressed out, animals can become tense, and clients can become frazzled. How you handle stress, deal with your own grief and loss, cope with the facets of grief, and balance your life and work situation is primary.

If grief is left unrecognized or your emotions unattended, (something covered in section 1), it can lead you to actually leaving a profession you once loved—without even realizing why.

I am sure you have experienced many astonishing and life-changing moments with animals. You probably have witnessed many delightful and loving moments between people and their beloved companions.

These moments are part of what keeps you going. They are the positive, healthy moments. These are the moments where death and grief opens the soul to profound and life-changing lessons. Death and grief due to death can be positive if we allow it to have its voice in a healthy way.

Together, as pet care professionals, let's join forces and talk about death and dying, pet loss grief, and the celebration of life differently. It's time for this conversation.

Warmly,

Wendy Van de Poll, MS, CEOL
June 17, 2017

Resources

Ways in which I can support you

Center for Pet Loss Grief: Through Life, Death, and Beyond
Wendy Van de Poll, MS, CEOL

A Free Gift from My Heart to Yours Awaits You!
https://centerforpetlossgrief.com

Free Pet Loss Grief Resources Packet
https://centerforpetlossgrief.com/pet-professional-grief-packet

Support for Pet Professionals
https://centerforpetlossgrief.com/pet-professional-grief-support

Online Courses for the Pet Professional and Pet Lover
https://spiritpaw.academy

Pet Grief Support
https://centerforpetlossgrief.com/pet-grief-support

Pet Funerals
https://centerforpetlossgrief.com/pet-funeral

Animal Mediumship
https://centerforpetlossgrief.com/animal-medium

Animal Communication
https://wendyvandepoll.com/animal-communication

Facebook
Center for Pet Loss Grief
https://facebook.com/centerforpetlossgrief

Pet Memorial Support Group
https://facebook.com/groups/petmemorials.
centerforpetlossgrief

Marley's Life Celebration Video
https://youtu.be/1bXUoPTivxk

Veterinarians

Veterinary Medical Association
http://ahvma.org

Home Euthanasia and Pet Hospice Veterinarians
http://iaahpc.org

Online Product Support:

BL Digital Media
https://bldigitalmedia.com/bl-life-celebration-videos/

Herbal Support: Pet Wellness Blends Affiliate
http://herbs-for-life-3.myshopify.com/#_l_1e

Magnetic Therapy Supplies: aVivoPur Affiliate
www.avivopur.com/#_a_CenterForPetLossGrief

Heart in Diamonds: Affiliate
http://www.heart-in-diamonds.com/?aff=CenterForPetLoss

Support Groups:

Association for Pet Loss and Bereavement
http://aplb.org

International Association for Animal Hospice and Palliative Care
http://iaahpc.org

Association for Human-Animal Bond Veterinarians
http://aahabv.org

Glossary

Burnout is a buildup of emotional exhaustion caused by an increase of stress that is not trauma-related. Oftentimes it causes social withdrawal.

Compassion fatigue is the emotional strain that a pet care professional will experience when working with a client suffering from traumatic events. It can occur with one client interaction or with cumulative client interactions.

End-of-life care aims to help animals live as well as possible and to die with dignity.

End-of-life safe means that you have a personal and professional plan for managing your emotional, physical, and spiritual health in order to process your experiences with grief and loss.

Good death is when a pet care professional is able to support a dying animal and relieve its suffering to provide the animal a peaceful way to leave this earth, whether it be through euthanasia or pet loss grief support.

Life celebration is a celebration of a pet's life that is personal and non-traditional with a focus on the memories of life with that particular pet.

Memorial board is a wall or board designed to preserve the memory of a pet. The theme could be a general timeline of special highlights of their life or a favorite and specific event. You can add photos, poems, etc. There is even software that you can use to make online slideshows. Please go to my resource section and see the memorial board that was done for my dog Marley.

Acknowledgments

First, I would love to express my deepest appreciation to all my fellow colleagues—the pet care professionals who dedicate their lives to doing the best they can every day even in the face of their own grief and loss. Thank you for sharing your stories and allowing yourself to express your grief—some of you for the first time.

I am truly in awe of my editor, Nancy Pile, who once again added her heart and paws to bring my book to another level. She brings my manuscripts to life! And thank you to Debbie Lum for her beautiful formatting and to Danijela Mijailovic for her gorgeous book cover artistry.

To Addie, Marley, Kado, Maya, and the rest of my fur, feather, and fin family who continue to hold my heart through the vital life lessons they impart and the goals they supply me as well, goals that I am determined to accomplish. They are amazing and wise teachers. They never let me forget who I am.

To my husband, Rick—helping me achieve my dreams. Love ya!

About the Author

Wendy Van de Poll is a pioneering leader in the field of pet loss grief support. Wendy is dedicated to providing a safe place for her clients to express their grief over the loss of their pets.

What makes Wendy successful with her clients is that she gets grief! As Wendy shared, "Over the years I've dealt with my own grief and helping many families communicate and connect with their pets long after their loss. It's what I've done since I was just 5 years old!"

She is compassionate and supportive to all who know her.

Wendy's passion is to help people when they are grieving over the loss of a pet. Her larger-than-life love for animals has led her to devote her life to the mission of increasing the quality of life between animals and people, no matter what stage they are in their cycle of life! She has been called the animal whisperer.

Wendy is a certified end-of-life and pet grief support coach, certified pet funeral celebrant, animal medium and communicator, and licensed massage therapist for human, horse and hound. She is the founder of The Center for Pet Loss Grief and an international best-selling and award-winning author and speaker.

Her courses are **AAVSB RACE**-certified, and she travels the country providing continuing education for veterinarian professionals.

Wendy holds a Master of Science in Wolf Ecology and Behavior, and has run with wild wolves in Minnesota, coyotes in Massachusetts, and foxes in her backyard. She lives in the woods with her husband, two crazy birds, her rescue dog Addie, and all kinds of wildlife.

Wendy currently has a Skype, phone, and in-person practice, providing end-of-life and pet grief support coaching, animal communication and mediumship, and personalized pet funerals.

You can reach her at www.centerpetlossgrief.com or www.wendyvandepoll.com.

Thank You for Reading

The Pet Professional's Guide to Pet Loss:

How to Prevent Burnout, Support Clients,
and Manage the Business of Grief

As the author of this book, I appreciate you buying and reading it. I hope that you found it to be helpful, as did the many others who shared their stories within its pages.

I would be grateful if you would leave a helpful book review, either with your favorite book distributor or with Amazon by going to http://a.co/67IxIof.

If you are interested in having me come to your practice to offer my **AAVSB RACE**-certified courses, please contact me at https://centerforpetlossgrief.com/contact.

Thank you,

Wendy Van de Poll, MS, CEOL
Best-selling Author
Certified End-of-Life and Pet Loss Grief Coach
Founder of The Center for Pet Loss Grief
AAVSB RACE-Certified

www.centerpetlossgrief.com
wendy@centerforpetlossgrief.com

Amazon Link for Pet Bereavement Books:

https://www.amazon.com/Wendy-Van-de-Poll/
e/B01BMUWX7O

The Pet Bereavement Series
Best Selling and Award Winning Books

By Wendy Van de Poll, MS, CEOL

My Dog IS Dying: What Do I Do?
My Dog HAS Died: What Do I Do?

My Cat IS Dying: What Do I Do?
My Cat HAS Died: What Do I Do?

Healing A Child's Pet Loss Grief

Free Book

Healing Your Heart From Pet Loss Grief

To receive notification when more books are published, please go to https://www.centerforpetlossgrief.com/, and we'll include you on the mailing list after you download your free gift.